BEGINNER'S GUIDE TO
COMMUNITY-BASED ARTS

Beginner's Guide to Community-Based Arts

Keith Knight, Lead Graphic Journalist
Ellen Forney, Graphic Journalist
Courtney Collins, Graphic Journalist
Rondell Crier, Graphic Journalist

Mat Schwarzman, Lead Author
William Cleveland, Editor

Christine Wong Yap, Art Director / Graphic Designer

BEGINNER'S GUIDE TO COMMUNITY-BASED ARTS

KEITH KNIGHT,
MAT SCHWARZMAN
AND MANY OTHERS

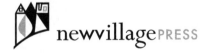

newvillagePRESS

New Village Press
New York, NY
hello@newvillagepress.net
www.newvillagepress.net

Printed in USA.
Second Edition, September, 2017.

Paperback
13-digit ISBN: 978-1-61332-024-2

Library of Congress Control Number: 2005929142

Cover design and interior layout by Christine Wong Yap.

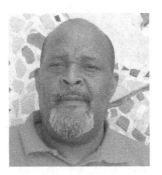

Dedicated to

James "Big Man" Maxton
(1947-2005)

of the Village of Arts and Humanities,
whose life is a testament to the
transformative power of
community-based arts.

This guide is also dedicated to the people and organizations whose stories are being told. They contributed enormous amounts of their time, energy and insight, as well as their art.

In addition, this guide is dedicated to the people whose stories are not being told, but who have traveled and are traveling the same journey toward the same destinations: peace, justice, equality, beauty. This includes the people of the East Bay Institute for Urban Arts in Oakland, CA (1994-2001) where the CRAFT framework was developed – the organization closed, but the work continues.

This guide is also dedicated to you, the reader. Hopefully, the richness of these few stories will inspire you to add your own story to the map. If you are a beginner, may this be just the first of many journeys...

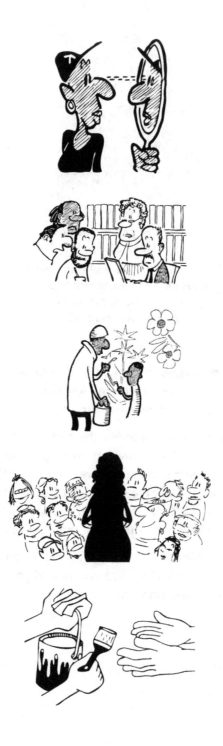

CONTENTS

PREFACE

Beginner's Guide to Community-Based Arts represents the stories of thousands of social change artists of all ages and backgrounds across the country and the globe. These amazing individuals and organizations work alongside students, teachers, workers, villagers, the unemployed, professionals, police officers, prisoners, government leaders, scholars, children and elders to tangibly transform their communities through art.

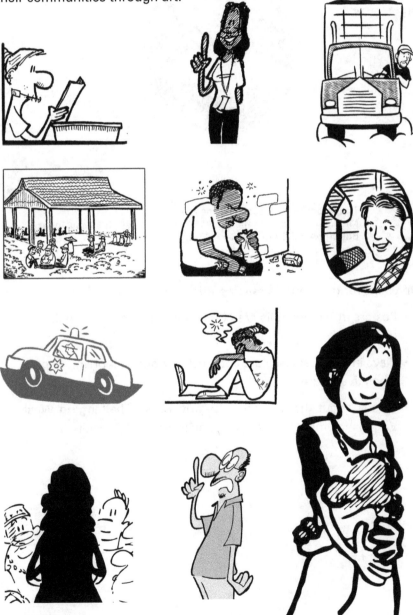

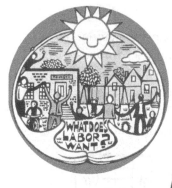

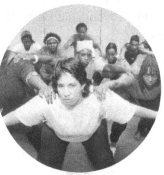

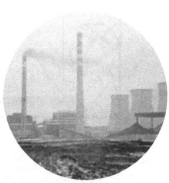

Top: A poster by Ricardo Levins Morales.
Middle: A detail from the profile of theater artist Rhodessa Jones.
Bottom: A still from a video by Tom Hansell.

On whatever day you are reading this, chances are:

- Posters in Minneapolis are **educating** workers about their rights.

- Plays in San Francisco are **convincing** women in prison to plan a positive future.

- Videos about the lives of truck drivers are **challenging** West Virginia lawmakers to re-think environmental policies.

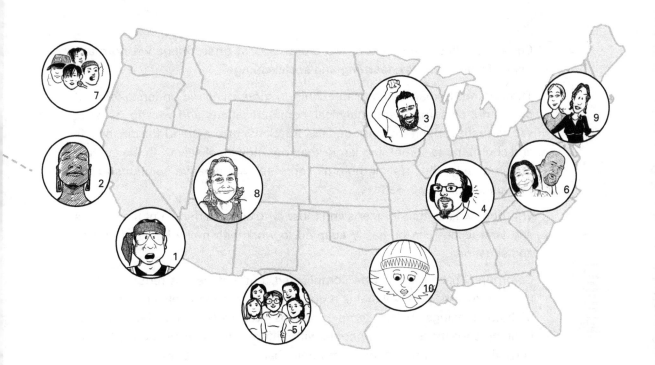

1 Chris Edaakie, Zuni Pueblo
2 Rhodessa Jones, San Francisco
3 Ricardo Levins Morales, Minneapolis
4 Tom Hansell, Kentucky / West Virginia
5 Mujer Artes, San Antonio
6 Village of Arts and Humanities, Philadelphia
7 Isang Mahal, Seattle
8 Tory Read, Denver
9 Picture Project, New York City / Internet
10 Young Aspirations / Young Artists, New Orleans

Drawing upon the stories of ten individuals and groups throughout the U.S., *Beginner's Guide to Community-Based Arts* provides a road map to the community-based art process. It offers **beginners** a general orientation, and **veterans** some time-tested routes they can use and pass on to others.

Community-based arts live at the crossroads of three things we normally think of separately: **art**, **learning** and **social change**.

Through art, human beings can acquire a more dynamic understanding of our world, plus important analytical, communications and vocational skills. We can reflect upon unconscious assumptions, take a stand for our beliefs and contribute to something larger than our individual selves. In the context of community, the arts can help us come up with creative solutions to the difficult social issues we face.

This book was written for teens and those who educate them, but these ideas and approaches can be easily adapted to work with many kinds of groups and situations.

Community-based art can be complicated, but it does not require special training to participate. All that is required is a determined belief in the power of human beings to overcome problems **creatively** and **collaboratively**. Building **consensus** among people with different perspectives, gifts, talents and skills is one of the things community-based art does best.

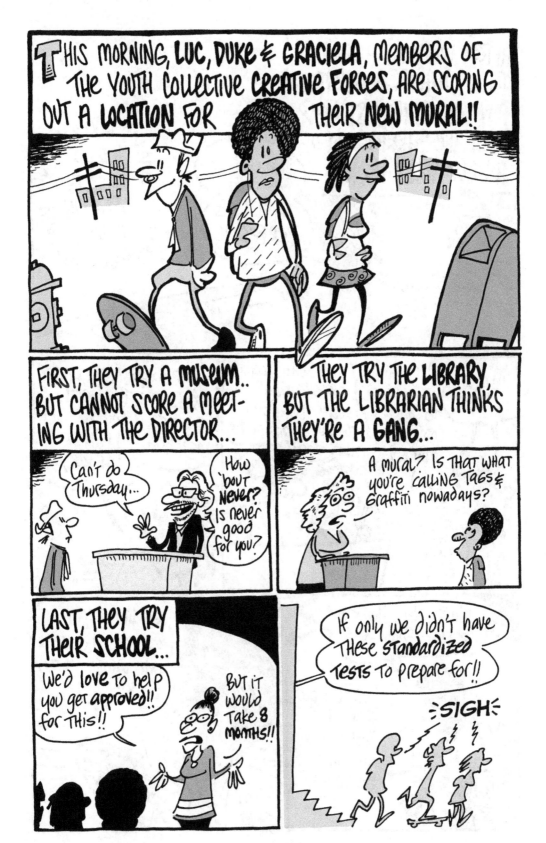

Art by Keith Knight, copyright 2017

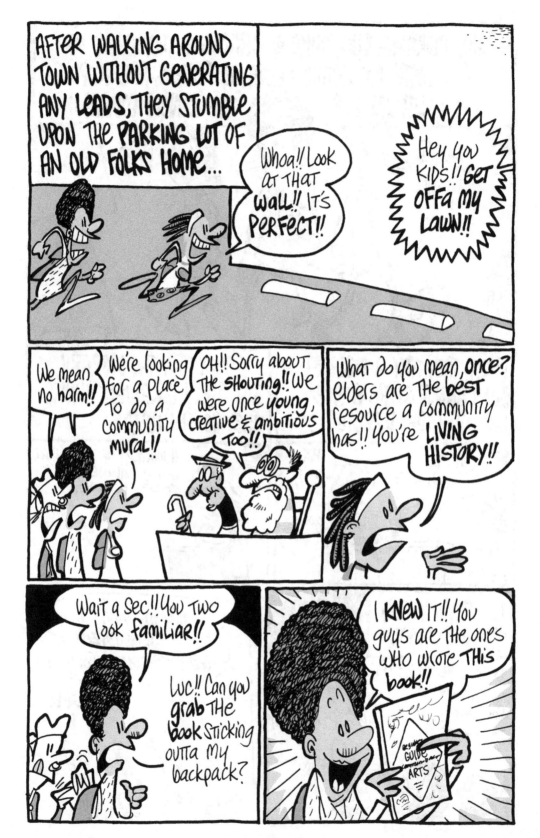

Art by Keith Knight, copyright 2017

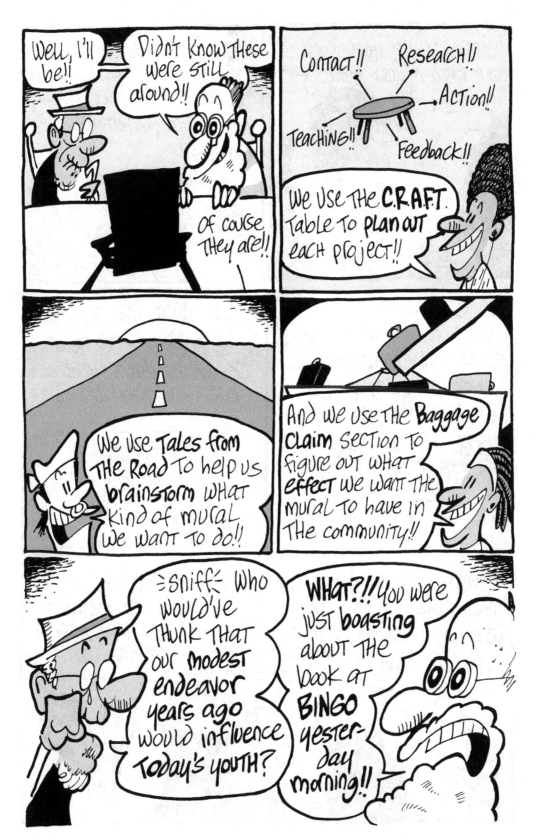

Art by Keith Knight, copyright 2017

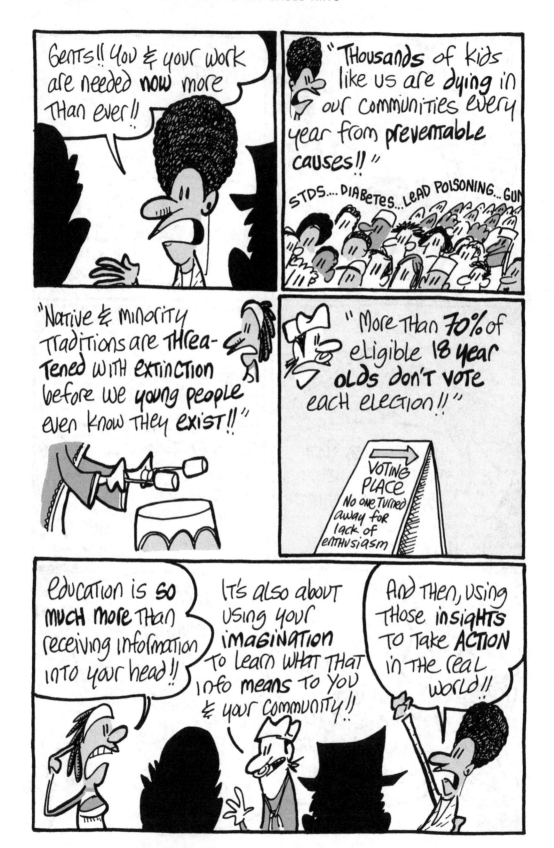

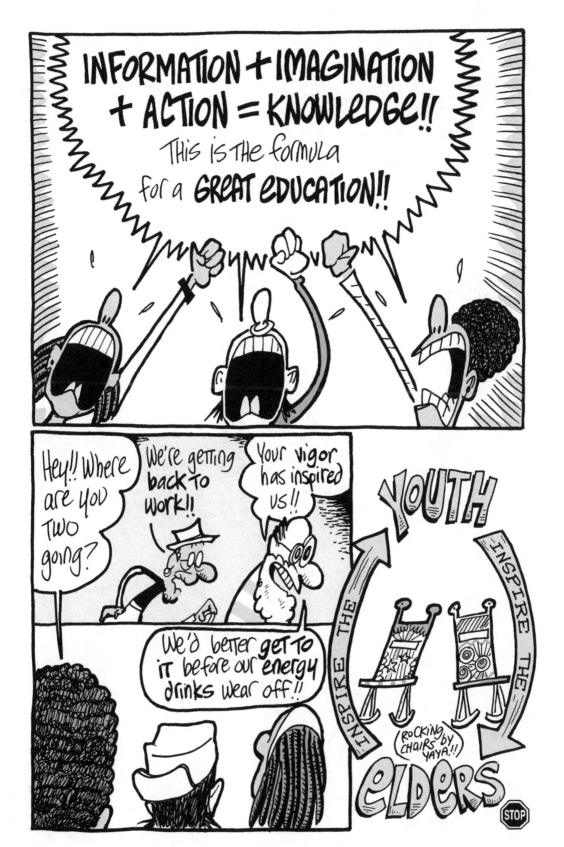

Art by Keith Knight, copyright 2017

PACKING FOR THE TRIP

Greetings!

My name is Mat Schwarzman. I am one of the authors and your guide. My job is to help you prepare for the journey, introduce you to each of the places we visit, and get you thinking about how you can lead activities in your own community.

Our journey will take us to five conceptual territories of the creative process: **Contact**, **Research**, **Action**, **Feedback** and **Teaching** (CRAFT). Within each territory, we will visit real-life places where people share a story about their successes, challenges, and lessons learned. Following each story, we go "inside the CRAFT Circle" to share related Tips, Topics and Techniques.

This guide can be useful at multiple points in the process, but, regardless of where you start, by the end of the journey you will gain new tools to navigate the community-based art process more effectively.

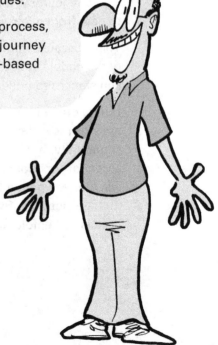

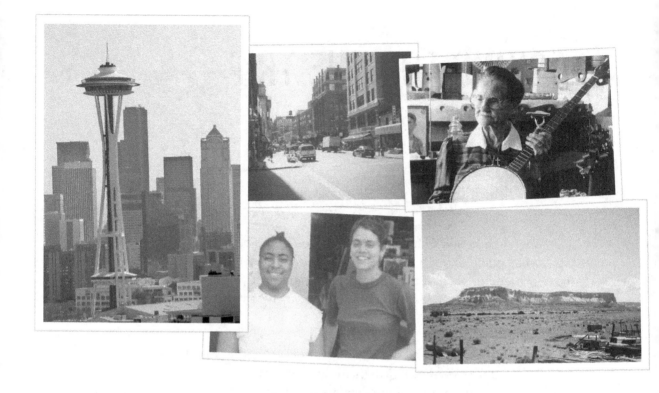

The guidebook uses the metaphor of a journey for several reasons:

First, because it mirrors the process we went through in creating this book.

Second, because every community-based art activity is like a journey, and as with any journey, things can get complicated and hard along the way. Better to hear from a few who have made the trip before.

Third, because community-based art arises from the specific circumstances of the people, places and time of its origin. You have to "travel" to those circumstances to understand the art.

During our journey, we will meet individuals and organizations across boundaries of race, class, artistic media, geography, cultural background, type of community, and community issue. Our travels will touch on almost every secondary school subject, including English, math, science, and social studies. You will gain a bird's eye view of the many thousands of new journeys that are possible. By the end of the trip, you will understand how the map itself is still unfolding.

MEET ME AT THE CROSSROADS

The image of the crossroads is central in many world cultures. To the Greeks, it is where the great tale of Oedipus begins and ends. To followers of Yoruba tradition, it is the home of Elegba, the god of destiny. In the Deep South of the United States, The Crossroads (an actual highway intersection in Mississippi) is where musician Robert Johnson sold his soul to the Devil so he could re-invent the blues.

Every true journey begins at a crossroads, a moment when the traveler asks: Where am I headed? Why am I doing this? Who am I to do this? And, How can I get some help? So, let us consider these questions ourselves before starting out.

Why read this guidebook? To find out how people across the United States are improving themselves and their communities through art.

Who is this for? Our journey is designed for teens, teachers, artists, and activists who engage in and facilitate community-based arts programs. However, this book is equally useful to researchers, city officials, arts councils, funders, policymakers, parents, and school administrators – in short, anyone involved in social change through the arts.

We anticipate this book will be most useful in middle and high schools, arts organizations, religious groups, youth development programs, social service agencies, universities, social action groups, community centers and street corners – wherever you find small groups (generally, fewer than 30) of teens and young people who are committed to a common project.

Where are we headed? To ten communities around the country where the community-based arts movement can be found.

How will the guidebook help? The book contains a wide range of resources to help you discover, imagine, and lead community-based arts projects. You will find lessons learned, project ideas, workshop exercises, links to the field and a map of the creative process you can use again and again.

As with any good journey, not everything will be laid out for you. Many of our "Tales from the Road," for example, are not primarily about young people. You will need to actively interpret and adapt the stories – we call them "parables of practice" – to fit your specific situations, needs and objectives.

GLOSSARY

You will need to know the meanings of some important words you will hear along the way. Most are commonly used words with specific meanings for the community-based arts journey.

art(s) Human behavior that involves the intense interpretation of life through language, dance, painting, music and numerous culturally specific forms.

community An interdependent group of people defined by a common place, intention, tradition, or spirit.*

community-based art Any form or work of art that emerges from a community and consciously seeks to increase the social, economic, and political power of that community.

consensus A group process for reaching a decision that integrates the interests and beliefs of all participants, and which all agree to support.

culture The structures and practices that human societies create to give order and meaning to their lives. This includes everything from beliefs and values to language, science, and art, as well as social customs, such as habits of eating, clothing, and recreation.

democracy A government based on the principle of equality, in which the people exercise power over public decisions to achieve the common good.

identity Characteristics humans use to structure and interpret one another's associations and interactions. Usually, ethnicity or race, social class, gender, religion, sexual preference, and age are considered major elements of identity.

learning The acquisition of knowledge coupled with an understanding of how that knowledge can be put to use.

objectives The positive effects that community-based arts activities can have upon participants and their communities. In this book, we focus on three broad areas: Art, Learning, and Social Change.

partnership (also referred to as **collaboration**) A give-and-take relationship based on mutual goals and objectives.

*This definition is inspired by Alternate ROOTS, one of the leading organizations serving the needs of community-based artists in the United States.

power The capacity to make and carry out decisions that affect one's life.

people power The capacity of people to unite on an issue and act to influence decisions and events that affect a community or the larger society.

social change Transformation in the formal and informal systems of society that lead to positive outcomes such as greater openness, equality and appreciation among people.

TYPES OF ACTIVITIES

program Ongoing, open-ended artistic project or series of projects.

project Series of workshops usually culminating in a finished artistic product.

workshops Exploratory sessions that involve artistic activity but may or may not lead toward a finished artistic product.

TYPES OF ROLES

community partners Organizations, such as social service agencies, schools, health centers, etc., who share needed resources, ideas, connections and expertise.

group (also referred to as **participants**) People from a community, such as neighbors, students, workers or others who participate as decision-makers in the planning, implementation and evaluation of activities, including the creation of art.

leader(s) An individual or group of individuals who are ready to act as organizers, mentors and educators in service to the group. Usually an artist, teacher and/or student with experience.

For more information on these concepts, see Trailblazers, p. 151.

A NEW LOOK

Next, you will need a new pair of conceptual "glasses" to see the world a bit differently. Looking through these glasses enables you to see something amazing: the basic human connection between art, learning and social change.

The following three concepts, or premises, form the lenses of these new glasses.*

PREMISE #1: CREATIVITY IS A MUSCLE

Creativity – that is, the use of the imagination to come up with a new idea or a different way to solve a problem – happens every day. The capacity to be creative is built into human beings at a biological level. Being creative is so natural, so basic to humanity, that very few of us even notice when we're doing it.

As a result, most people don't realize creativity can be practiced. What Western society calls "art" is, in actuality, a language of cultural codes and behaviors to help human beings develop their creativity both individually and collectively. While many people (mainly adults) say "I haven't an artistic bone in my body," creative ability is always there – like a muscle – to be developed and strengthened in each person as an integral part of their lives, throughout their lives. The more you practice, the more creative you can become.

The people we call "artists" are those who exercise, apply and hone their creative muscles regularly through one or more artistic disciplines, such as theater, painting, music, multimedia, poetry and sculpture. **Actors** study how the voice and body communicate feelings. **Painters** study color, light and composition. **Videomakers** study motion, rhythm, sound.

In reality, being an artist is similar to being an athlete. Some are professional, some are amateurs, some are geniuses, but their basic skills all require continuous practice.

*For information on the research behind the three premises, see Credits, p. 165.

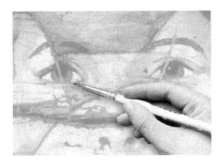
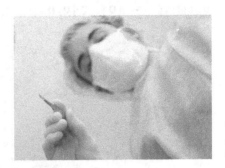

The skills
of art are the
skills of life.

The basic skills of the artist – imitation, composition, expression – are fundamental to our daily lives. The lawyer in the courtroom, the sales person in the commercial, the waiter in the restaurant, all call upon some of the same skills as actors to communicate effectively. Surgeons, engineers, and even police officers have to visualize and make sense of objects in space just as painters do. People who work in advertising utilize the same principles of composition, design, and iconography as choreographers and graphic designers. And when composers create harmonies they use the same part of the brain as mathematicians and software developers.

Creativity is more than just useful, it is the critical human survival skill. Without it, human beings are perhaps the weakest, slowest and most vulnerable species on the planet. Every day, human beings must be able to deal effectively with situations using little else but their skills of creative interpretation and improvisation. Creativity gives us a chance to select and refine the best, most effective ways of responding to life – a chance to plan and prepare for the future.

One key to leading effective community-based arts activities is to approach a group as a coach approaches a team of athletes. Your job as a leader is to:

- Discover and develop each participant's unique abilities.

- Coordinate and focus these abilities so the group can flex its creative muscles on behalf of the community.

PREMISE #2: ART IS INFORMATION

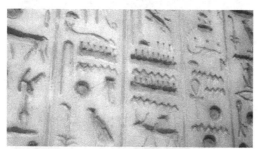

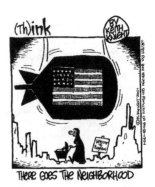

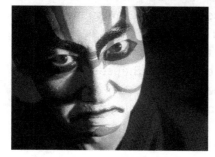

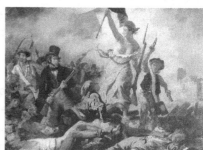

Our most important ideas and experiences are conveyed through artistic means.

To many people, art exists in a separate fantasy universe, with each art form its own planet (The Film World, The Painting World, The Poetry World, etc.). In reality, art is very much a part of everyday life on Earth.

Every building, car, advertisement and piece of furniture we encounter has been designed using artistic principles. Everywhere we turn, from our most public to our most private living environments, our world is filled with forms of expression that use music, movement, drama, and design.

But it doesn't stop here. All our major social systems – government, commerce, religion – rely on the same language as the arts in order to convey information. Representatives are elected through a formalized ritual known as "voting", police wear dark blue outfits symbolizing "the law," and products are sold to us through 30-second dramas called "commercials." We even greet one another using a very theatrical gesture known as "the handshake." Why?

Since the beginnings of humanity, we have had to encode our most vital information so that we could remember and elaborate upon it in light of current circumstances. Art or, more precisely, the language of art is how

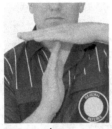
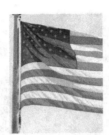
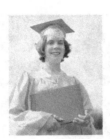
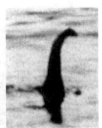

signs   symbols   rituals   stories

Four types of
cultural codes.

we accomplish this. At each important moment of life – birth, adulthood, graduation, marriage, retirement, death – we act artistically in order to investigate, reflect upon and advance what is most important to us. As society becomes more complex and the storehouse of human knowledge grows, we rely increasingly on these codes to capture, reinforce and transfer ideas, information, history, values, and beliefs to others, especially younger generations.

These are four basic types of cultural codes:

signs Images or actions that communicate vital information and often require immediate responses, like "stop," "flip this switch for power," and "hamburgers inside."

symbols Images or actions representing commonly held abstract concepts (values, beliefs, ideas) that have risen up over time. Religious symbols such as the cross or the Star of David are obvious examples.

rituals Events or actions that involve repeated, formal acts and are prescribed by social tradition. Flag ceremonies and parades, for example, are rituals that occur in many human societies and cultures.

stories The use of language to forge real and imagined experiences into coherent, meaningful narratives.

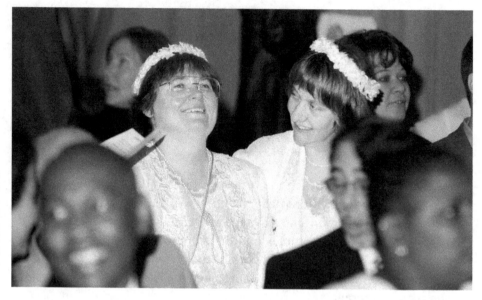

Cultural codes help define social roles. Here, a couple in San Francisco wait for a "domestic partner ceremony" to begin.

PREMISE #3: COMMUNITIES ARE CULTURES

"Community" is as basic to humans as "flock" is to birds. Humans are designed for communal living. Our ancestors began to walk upright in large part from the desire for greater social interaction.

Communities and community organizations are basic units of human survival, so the ability of individuals to come together as communities is essential. As the saying goes "It takes a village to raise a child." The reality is it takes a village to do just about anything.

There is no rule about how many people constitute a community. However, it is worth noting that human beings have spent most of history (over three million years) in communities of about 100. Even today, while communities in the U.S. shift much more than they used to, most of us still depend upon a consistent core network of about that many people for our daily survival.

The concept of community is so deeply embedded in the human character, it is hard to define. In many languages, the word for "community" is the same as the word for "us" and "people." The concept can be applied to family, friends and neighborhood, a town or country, even the planet. Many people, when they visualize community, see a location, yet some of the world's oldest communities (such as the Bedouins) and newest communities (on the Internet) are not based at a single physical site.

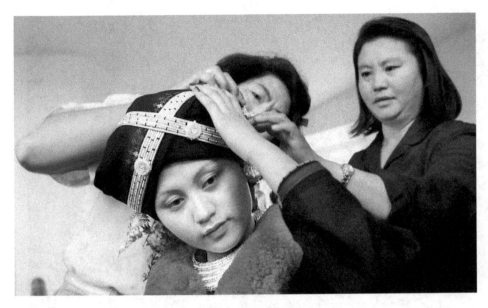

Cultural codes can stimulate interaction and appreciation between generations. Here, a Mien American girl is prepared for a community performance by her elders.

All communities have cultural codes to signify their most important shared agreements and values – "I will cross at the crosswalk because that's where drivers agree to stop for pedestrians," "I will go to school because I believe it leads to a more fulfilling career," etc.

These codes include many things, from team mascots (Go, Bulldogs!) to historical community incidents (Were you around when...) to maps (That's where the river is) to well known individuals. Cultural codes can be expressed through a song, a statue, a phrase, or any image that sparks strong feelings and associations.

Cultural codes are powerful. They shape our thoughts, our dreams, what groups we identify with, everything down to our most basic sense of reality.

For most of human history, these codes evolved *locally* through ethnic and family ties, schools, workplaces, friendships, religious and civic organizations. But over the last two centuries, since the advent of mass media, cultural codes have been controlled *remotely* by private universities, government agencies, and corporate networks.

All art calls upon these cultural codes in some way, but through community-based art people consciously take ownership of their signs, symbols, rituals

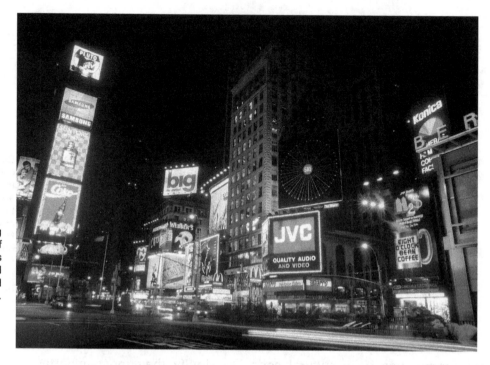

A growing
number of
cultural codes
are created
and controlled
remotely.

and stories in order to re-connect and extend their sense of common ground. Out of common ground comes learning, and from learning comes the power of human beings to transform society and social life for the better – what we call "people power."

In today's world, it can take a problem or injustice, a bad economy or the need for better schools, for people to rediscover their sense of people power – this is where community-based arts often come into play.

But whether it is a week-long workshop, a year-long project or a permanent program, the skills enhanced through community-based arts have the potential to go beyond fixing problems to developing solutions. This ability to unleash our "social imagination" – to help us envision the world differently – makes community-based arts a uniquely important type of social change strategy.

LET'S GO!

One more thing you will need is a conceptual map to help you carry what you learn on the journey back to your own communities. The map we use is called "CRAFT" and it stands for five territories of the community-based art process:

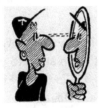

CONTACT
Cultivate trust, mutual understanding and commitment as a foundation for your creative partnership.

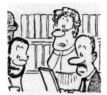

RESEARCH
Gather information about the people, places and issues you are working with.

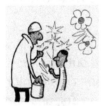

ACTION
Produce a new work of art that benefits the community.

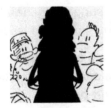

FEEDBACK
Spark community reflection, dialogue and organizing to spread the impact of the new work.

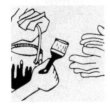

TEACHING
Pass on new community-building skills to others to sustain the impact.

Each of these five territories has its own section or chapter of stories in the guidebook. Together they represent a complete creative journey.

As we travel through each of the territories, I will be there to help you get the most out of the journey.

- Following each story, we go Inside the CRAFT Circle to find Tips, Topics and Techniques gathered from working artists, educators and activists across the country.

- Following the last story, I'll show you Resources to help you follow up on the stories, issues and approaches that are most interesting to you. These Resources include Trailblazers, Artist Profiles, Links to the Field, CRAFT Activities Table, and a Sample CRAFT Program Design.

- Once you finish reading the guidebook, join our online learnng community (The C.R.A.F.T. Circle) to share your ideas and meet other artist-educator activists: **www.thecraftcircle.org**

Finally, before we head out, here are two last pieces of advice to remember on your way.

- These ten parables of practice are real stories, told by the people who lived them. They are not necessarily pretty or funny, but they are useful, and they offer profound examples of personal and community transformation. Several of the stories span months, years, and some more than a decade. They are all specific, yet each suggests general insights that apply across communities, artistic disciplines, and issues.

- The stories do not always translate into easy answers or step-by-step instructions. Rather, they demonstrate the promise and possible pitfalls you are likely to encounter in a community-based art project.

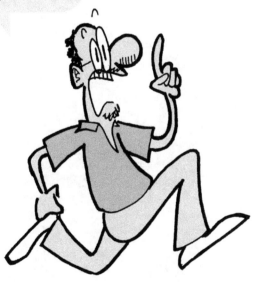

TALES FROM THE ROAD

CONTACT

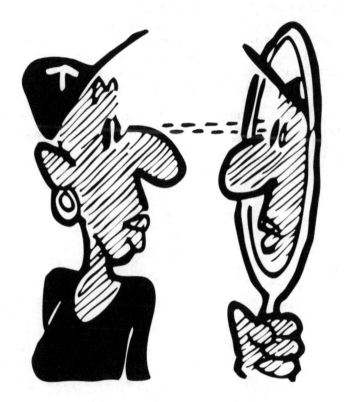

Cultivate trust, mutual understanding
and commitment as a foundation
for your creative partnership.

Welcome!

We are in **Contact** territory, the first of five territories
of the community-based arts process.

Contact is the place where you and your group begin
exploratory workshops and interactions with the community.
Here, the group takes stock of their experiences, assets,
assumptions and expectations.

Anxiety-producing questions can come up, like:
Am I good enough? Creative enough? Committed enough?
Can I get along with all these people?
This is also the time when basic group decisions need to be made.
Which art forms and styles are we using?
What issues and themes are we going to investigate?
And even more basic, How are we going to behave with each other?

It's a lot, and you as a leader need to be simultaneously *aware* of the
challenges and *confident* the group will meet them all successfully.

Listen to the people we're about to visit. They will help us begin
thinking about and planning for success.

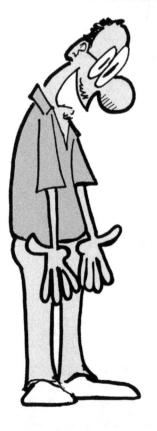

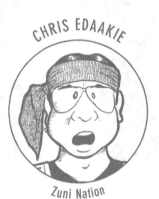

CHRIS EDAAKIE

Zuni Nation

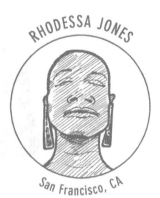

RHODESSA JONES

San Francisco, CA

Hey, we're slowing down.
We must be arriving at
the first stop!

Our first destination lies a few miles off the famous "Route 66" in northwestern New Mexico in one of the oldest and most traditional communities in North America –

Zuni Pueblo.

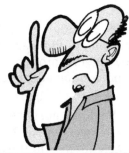

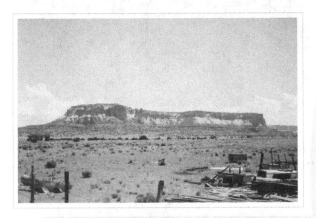

For more than 900 years, the Zuni people (who call themselves the "A:shiwi") have lived under the watchful eye of their sacred Corn Mountain.

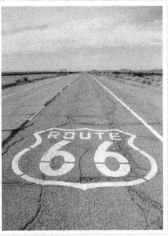

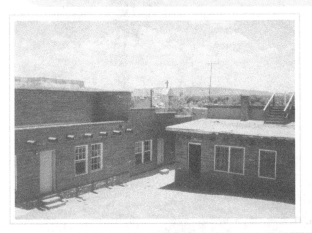

For most of that time, the Zuni have been known throughout the region for their abilities as farmers, hunters and gatherers. Working in the harsh soils and waters of this rocky mountain plateau, the Zuni had an intimate and widely envied relationship with nature.

But now, like many communities in the United States, the Zuni are faced with an epidemic of staggering proportions –

diabetes.

One half of all Zuni adults over age 50 currently have the disease.

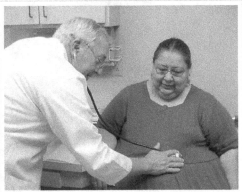

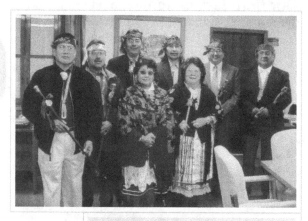

In 1998, the Zuni Tribal Council began a long-term campaign to reduce diabetes through grassroots prevention education.

The Healthy Lifestyles program uses Zuni stories, signs, symbols and rituals to motivate changes in living habits that improve the health of all 10,000 residents.

Contact with community is central to this life-saving program, that begins at birth and extends through eldercare.

And the approach works – within a few short years, the terrible statistics are beginning to improve.

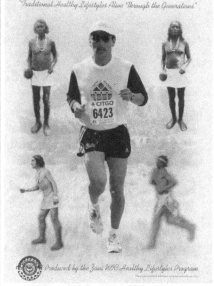

What makes Healthy Lifestyles so effective?

One important element is their cadre of amazing bilingual/bicultural teens who serve as 21st Century artist-educator-activists.

Let's find out how they make Contact in the story we call **"I-Am-Going-But-I-Shall-Return."**

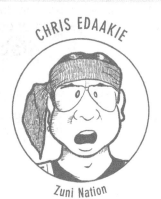

CHRIS EDAAKIE

Zuni Nation

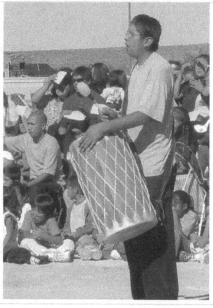

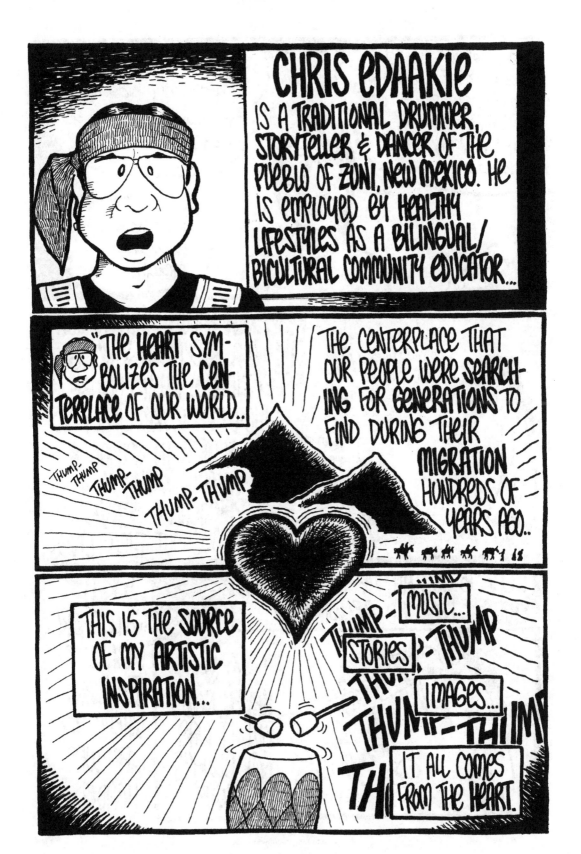

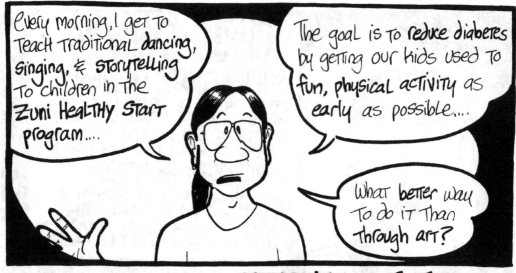

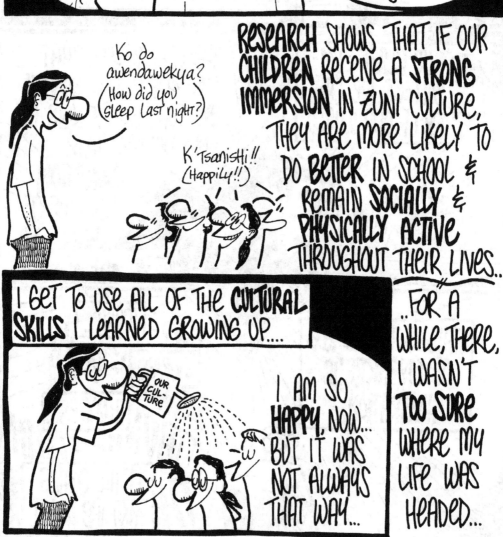

Art by Keith Knight, copyright 2005

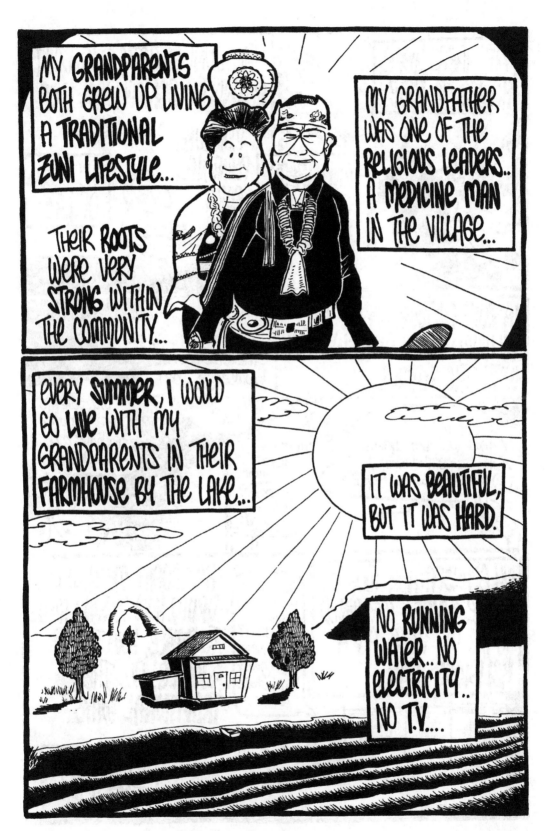

Art by Keith Knight, copyright 2005

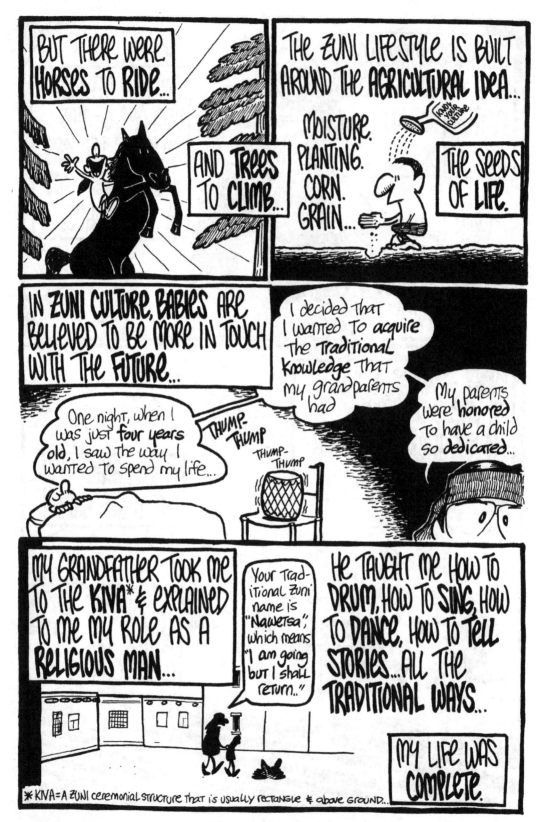

Art by Keith Knight, copyright 2005

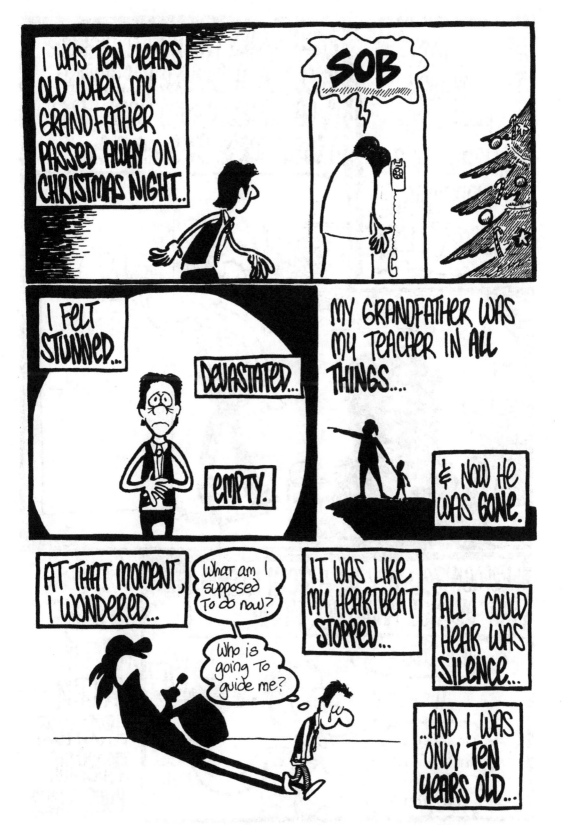

Art by Keith Knight, copyright 2005

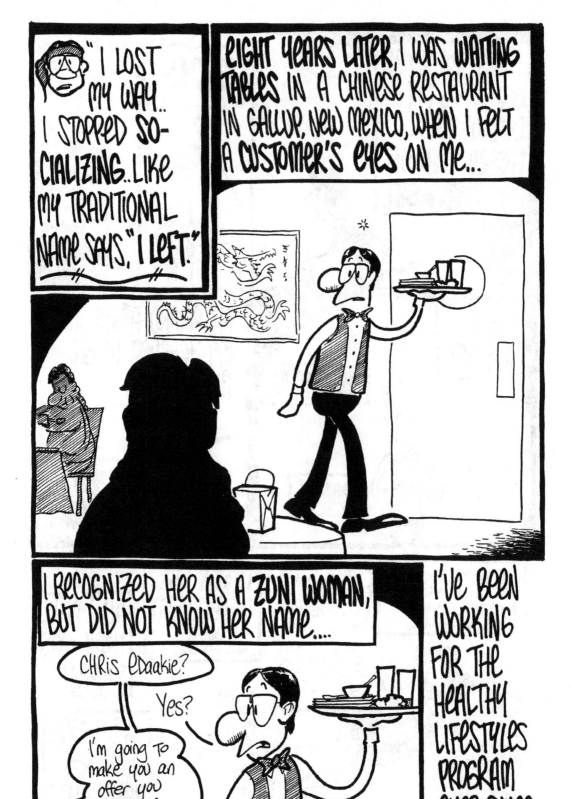

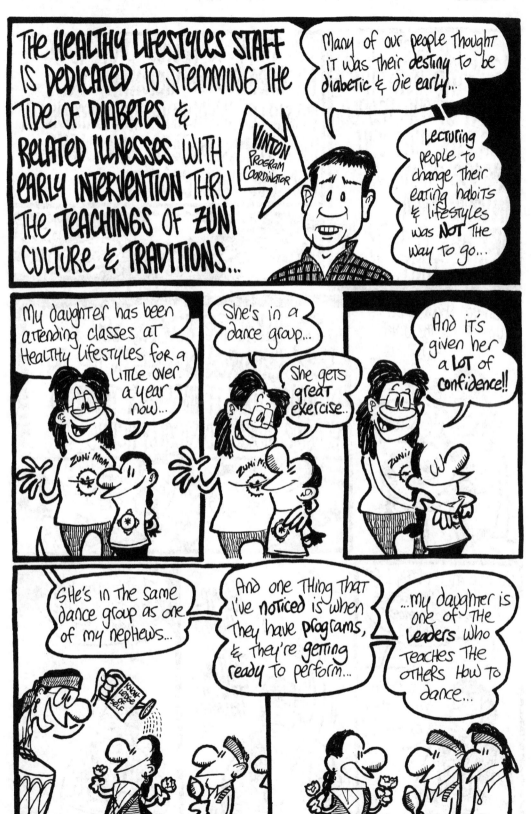

Art by Keith Knight, copyright 2005

"WE NEEDED TO TAP INTO THE **HEART** OF OUR PEOPLE IN A WAY THAT WILL ENGAGE THEM... INVOLVE THEM... **ART** HAS A WAY OF DOING THAT...."

THE STAFF IS RELIED UPON TO BE AS **CREATIVE** & **VISIONARY** AS POSSIBLE.. INVOLVING THE COMMUNITY WITH FLIERS, POSTERS, GIVEAWAYS AND **CULTURAL** EVENTS...

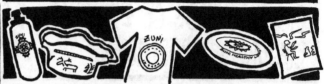

Can you show what you teach the other kids?

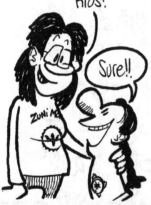

Sure!!

"WHEN THE ELDERS SEE THE CHILDREN DANCING IN THE TRADITIONAL WAY, IT INSPIRES THEM TO BECOME MORE PHYSICALLY ACTIVE...."

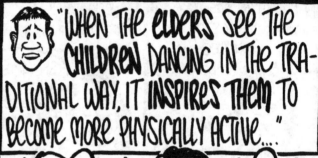

THUMP THUMP

We here at HEALTHY Life-styles take the issues our people care **most** about...

"..& connect with them **artistically**...

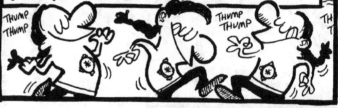

THUMP-THUMP

THUMP-THUMP

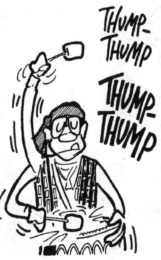

That is the key to finding the heartbeat.

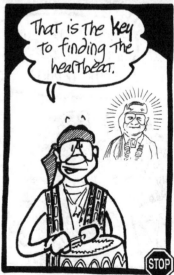

STOP

Art by Keith Knight, copyright 2005

INSIDE THE CRAFT CIRCLE

TIP

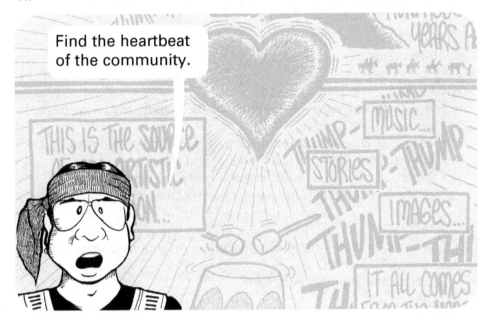

TOPICS

- *Where* are the special places in your community where people gather when they want to celebrate? protest? mourn?
- *When* are the special days of the year when people in your community gather to celebrate? protest? mourn?
- *What* might represent the heartbeat of your community?
- *How* does the heart of your community beat in you?

TECHNIQUE: CULTURAL INVENTORY WORKSHOP
Derived from exercises of the East Bay Institute for Urban Arts, Oakland, CA

DURATION
15–25 minutes

OBJECTIVES
- Art: Gather information about the cultural assets and capacities of the group.
- Learning: Discuss connections between cultural preferences and ethnicity, family background, gender and class.
- Social Change: Build trust between members of the group from different backgrounds in preparation for collaboration.

MATERIALS
- Electronic Device for each student (computer, smartphone, tablet)
- Internet/LAN Access
- Projector and Screen/Smartboard

IN ADVANCE
- Reproduce or adapt the template on the next page as a survey using the cloud (e.g. Google Drive, Poll Anywhere) or an email attachment (e.g. Microsoft Word).
- If you do not have enough electronic devices, create and print out a paper version of the survey so that all participants can answer the questions simultaneously.

STEPS
1. Introduce the activity by talking about the concept of cultural assets and how it relates to personal and social power.

2. Instruct participants to complete the survey as quickly as possible without too much thinking (you are not looking for "the" favorite, just "a" favorite).

3. Once everyone is done, ask participants to share some of their results.

4. Facilitate one large group or multiple small group brainstorms about how overlapping and complementary preferences and skills could be used as the basis for collaborative artistic products.

FOLLOW-UP
- Use notes from the brainstorming to choose art forms, products, etc.
- Use the survey data to construct a "Cultural Jeopardy" board for the group to play together using the headings Signs, Symbols, Rituals and Stories.
- Have participants ask family members and friends the same questions and share the results in the group.

NOTE
- Works well as the opening activity for a collaborative planning process.

CULTURAL INVENTORY TEMPLATE

Full Name	
Nickname(s)	
A Favorite Book	
A Favorite Song	
A Favorite Dance or Dance Type	
A Favorite Joke	
A Favorite Work of Visual Art	
A Favorite Movie	
A Favorite Sport	
A Favorite Food	
A Favorite Piece of Clothing	
A Favorite Place	
A Favorite Holiday	
A Favorite Ceremony	
A Favorite Historical Figure	
A Favorite Group You Are In	
A Favorite Family Member	
A Favorite Talent	
A Favorite Collection	

For our next story, we go to

San Francisco, California.

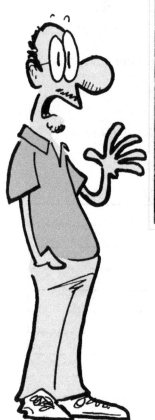

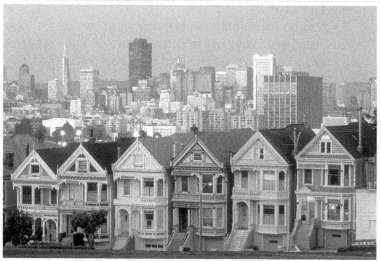

The 13th largest city in the United States, with its picturesque hills, moderate weather and stunning ocean views, San Francisco is considered by many to be the most beautiful city on earth.

And yet, even with all this beauty, there are serious problems.

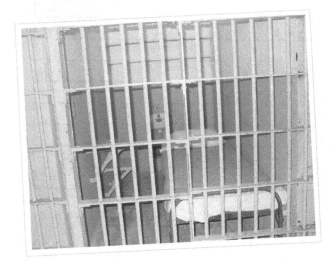

In California, the Golden State, the prison population has risen 800% in the last 25 years, making the California prision system one of the world's largest.

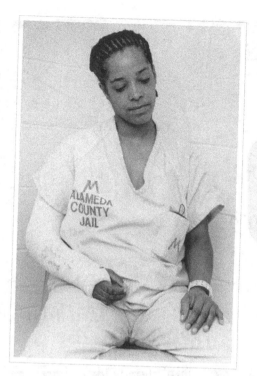

In San Francisco (as in most of the US), the rate of growth for female inmates has exceeded that of male inmates each year since 1981.

Women of African American and Latin American descent are five times more likely than European American women to spend time in jail at some point in their lives.

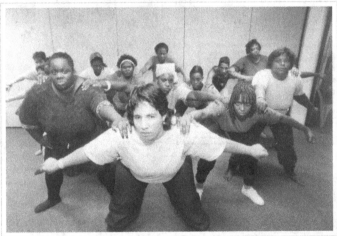

Dancer, actress, singer and playwright **Rhodessa Jones** did not know what to expect her first day as an artist-in-residence in the San Francisco County Jail at San Bruno.

But she set aside her personal assumptions, and as a result a new theater company was created that has since helped hundreds of women exit the revolving door of prison life.

Here's her story...
"More Than Aerobics."

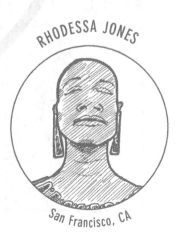

RHODESSA JONES

San Francisco, CA

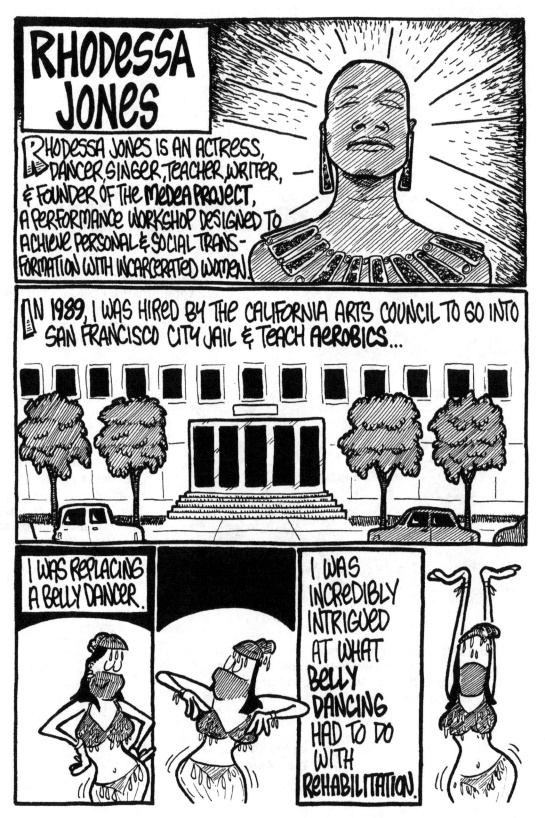

RHODESSA JONES

RHODESSA JONES IS AN ACTRESS, DANCER, SINGER, TEACHER, WRITER, & FOUNDER OF THE MEDEA PROJECT, A PERFORMANCE WORKSHOP DESIGNED TO ACHIEVE PERSONAL & SOCIAL TRANSFORMATION WITH INCARCERATED WOMEN!

IN 1989, I WAS HIRED BY THE CALIFORNIA ARTS COUNCIL TO GO INTO SAN FRANCISCO CITY JAIL & TEACH AEROBICS...

I WAS REPLACING A BELLY DANCER.

I WAS INCREDIBLY INTRIGUED AT WHAT BELLY DANCING HAD TO DO WITH REHABILITATION.

Art by Keith Knight, copyright 2005

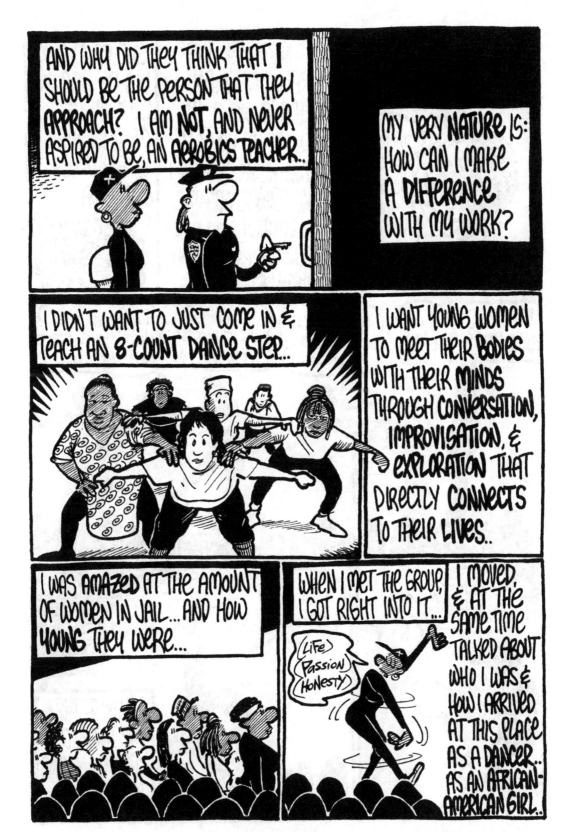

Art by Keith Knight, copyright 2005

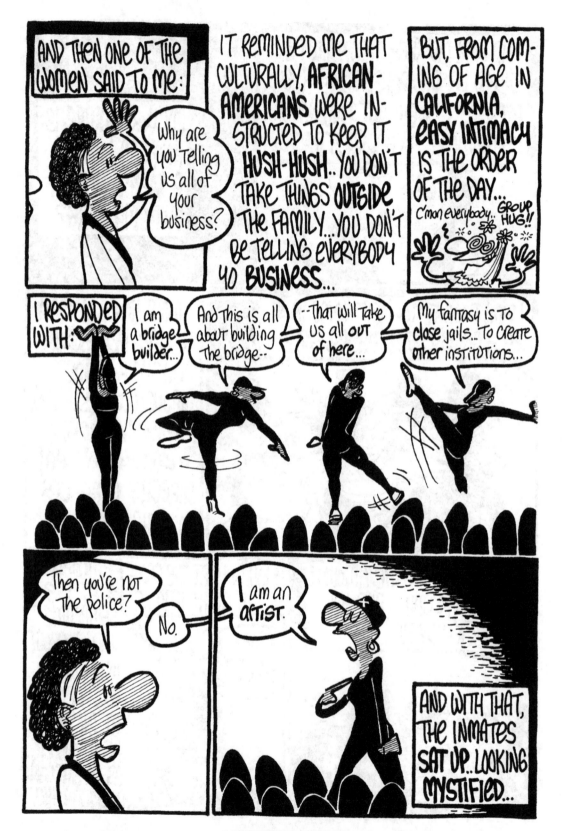

Art by Keith Knight, copyright 2005

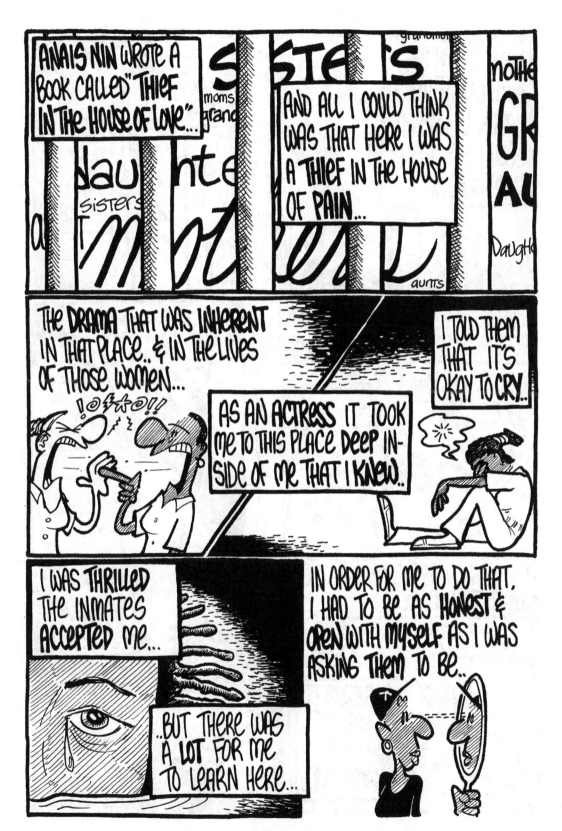

Art by Keith Knight, copyright 2005

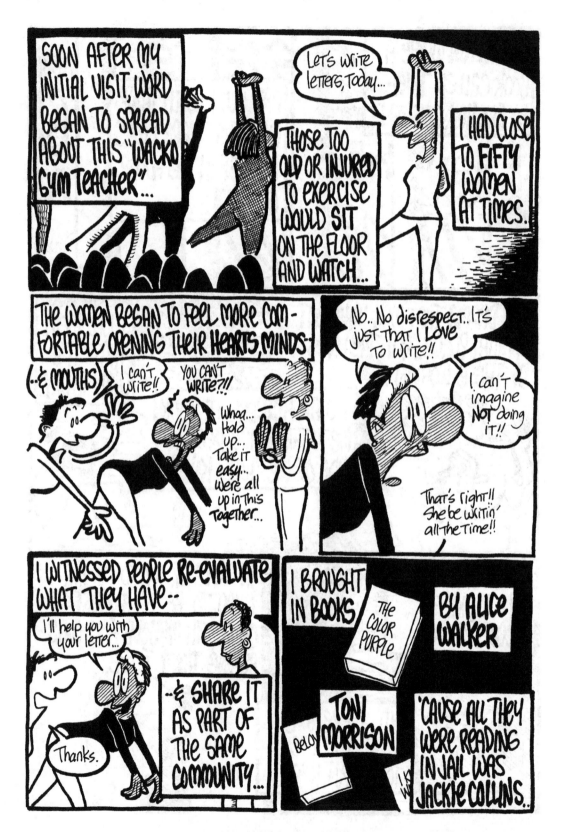

Art by Keith Knight, copyright 2005

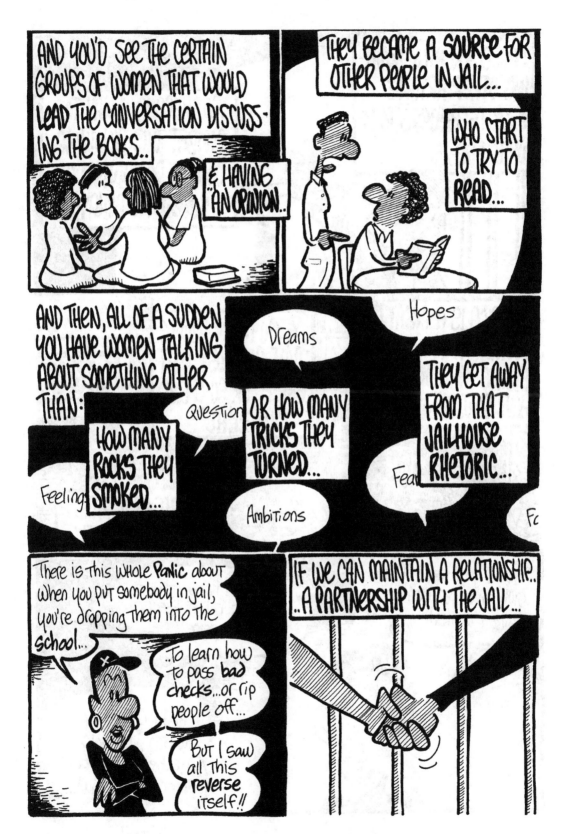

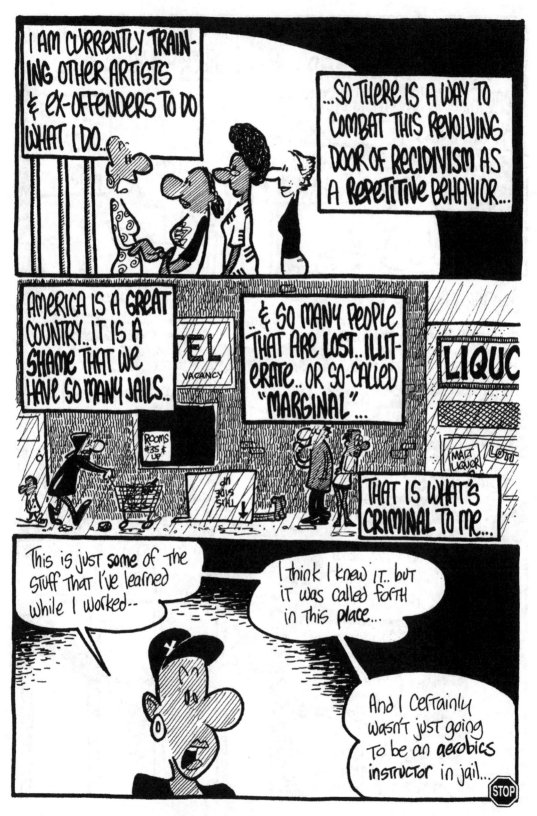

Art by Keith Knight, copyright 2005

INSIDE THE CRAFT CIRCLE

TIP

Be as honest and open with yourself as you are asking others to be.

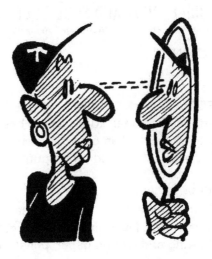

TOPICS

- Why might people in a community resist participating in a project?
- What personal barriers might get in the way of open communication?
- What assumptions might you have about a community and its people?
- What common goals do you and the people in the community share?

TECHNIQUE: BODY AND SOUL / BODY AND SOUND EXERCISE
Derived from exercises of Rhodessa Jones, San Francisco, CA

DURATION
   1 to 2 hours

OBJECTIVES
   • Art: Use personal stories as the basis for artistic expression.
   • Learning: Establish personal learning and developmental goals.
   • Social Change: Build group purpose and unity.

MATERIALS
   • A quiet space where the group can move freely
   • Tape or CD player and a piece of contemplative music
   • Drawing and writing paper, pens/pencils (distributed in advance)

STEPS
   1. Ask participants to find a place in the room to lie on their backs (shoes off and eyes closed).

   2. Play an excerpt of the selected music, and verbally encourage the group to imagine themselves five years in the future.

   3. After 10 minutes, ask everyone to draw something using the music as inspiration.

   4. Display the drawings on the wall.

   5. Ask participants to view each other's work and write their response to each drawing.

   6. Invite participants to share excerpts of their writing with the group.

   7. Discuss how the exercise helped to cultivate trust and understanding in the group, and what common goals emerged.

VARIATIONS & EXTENSIONS
   • Use the writings as a source for composing lyrics, poetry, monologues, etc.
   • Help participants develop a contract with themselves and the group to pursue the visions that come out of this exercise.

RESEARCH

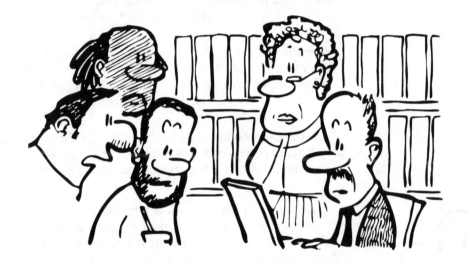

Gather information about the people,
places and issues you are working with.

Welcome to the second territory, **Research.**

If Contact can be thought of as looking inward, then Research is about looking outward. Here, the focus is on listening, observing and learning from others beyond your immediate community.

In order to conduct effective Research, a group must be prepared to get systematic about itself and its goals. Participants will need to take specific areas of responsibility. Different types of information will be needed such as:

From the Art side: What images, phrases, stories, places are related to our theme? What are some examples of effective art works in this form and/or on this theme? What makes them effective?

From the Community side: Who are the people and institutions affected? How are they affected? What are the histories behind the issues? Who makes the decisions and how?

As leader, it will be your job to keep the group moving together and focused on its Research objectives. In the heat of a creative process, this can be difficult to do. Research can be grueling at times, and participants may have the impulse to begin Action (in other words, complete and present an artistic product) too quickly.

Take the time to conduct good, thorough Research in the community. Your art and your impact will benefit.

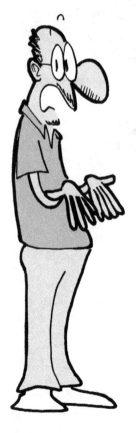

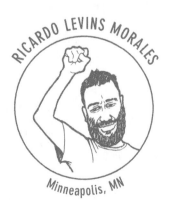

RICARDO LEVINS MORALES

Minneapolis, MN

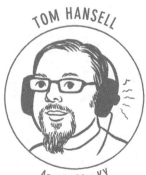

TOM HANSELL

Appalachia, KY

Next, we visit the midwestern city of

Minneapolis, Minnesota...

...(population 400,000), known for its stunning lakes, freezing cold winters and free-thinking ways.

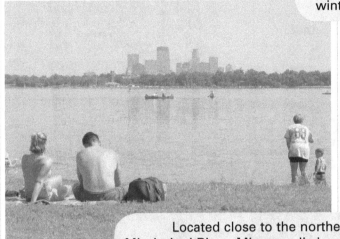

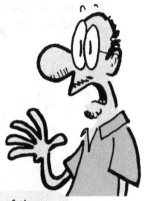

Located close to the northern source of the Mississippi River, Minneapolis is a major thoroughfare where thousands of truckers and dockworkers move goods to and from other parts of the country.

Not surprising then, Minneapolis has also been home to labor unionists and labor activism.

In 1934, two hundred Minneapolis Teamsters walked out on their jobs, leading to a restructuring of labor-corporate relations throughout the U.S.

In the 1980s, a strike by meat-packers in nearby Austin, Minnesota led to a national restructuring of relations between union members and union leadership.

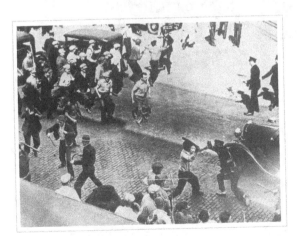

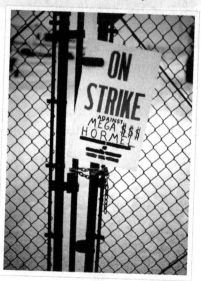

Labor unions have been central to
our democratic culture, but...

Who takes responsibility for gathering
and passing on union culture?

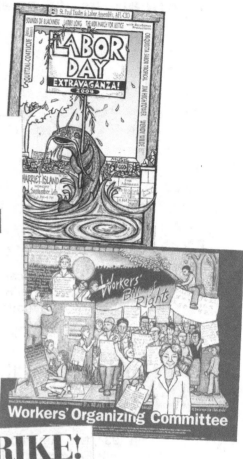

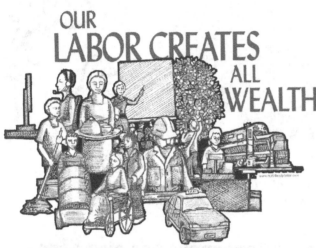

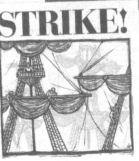

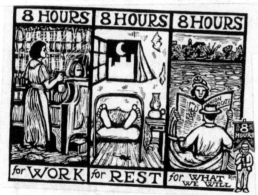

Who makes sure
the people of Minneapolis
remember that unions are
"the people who brought
you the weekend"?

Meet **Ricardo Levins Morales**,
a union artist who draws inspiration
from the signs, symbols and stories of
his community, in "Visual Griot."

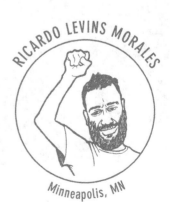

shaman *n.*: A member of certain tribal societies who acts as a medium between the visible & the spirit worlds, practicing magic or sorcery for purposes of healing, divination & control over natural events...

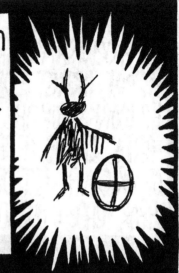

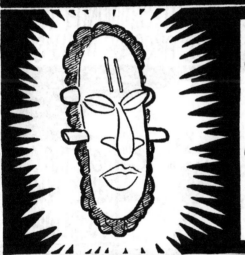

griot *n.*: a storyteller in Western Africa who perpetuates the oral tradition and history of a village or family...

THIS IS THE STORY OF A DIFFERENT TYPE OF GRIOT...

A DIFFERENT TYPE OF SHAMAN...

ONE WHO TELLS STORIES & HEALS COMMUNITIES--

--THROUGH PICTURES.

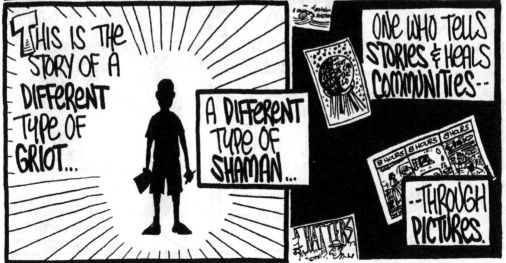

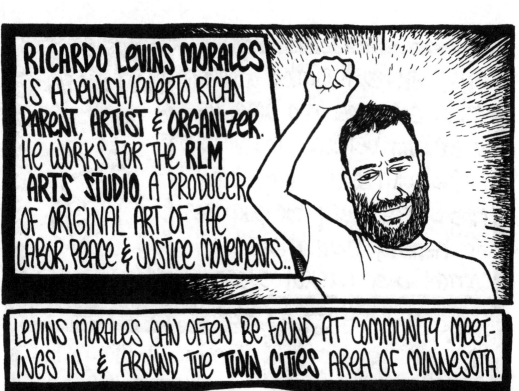

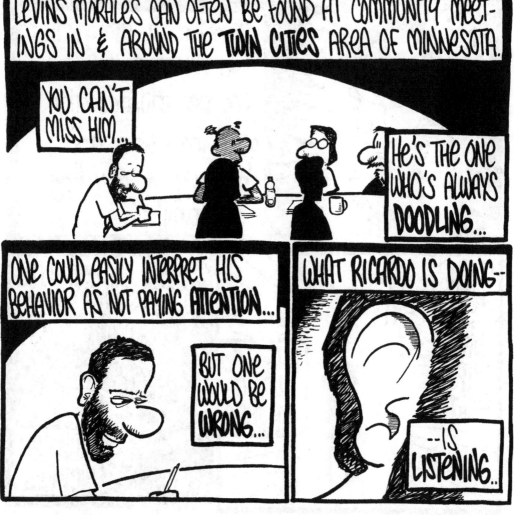

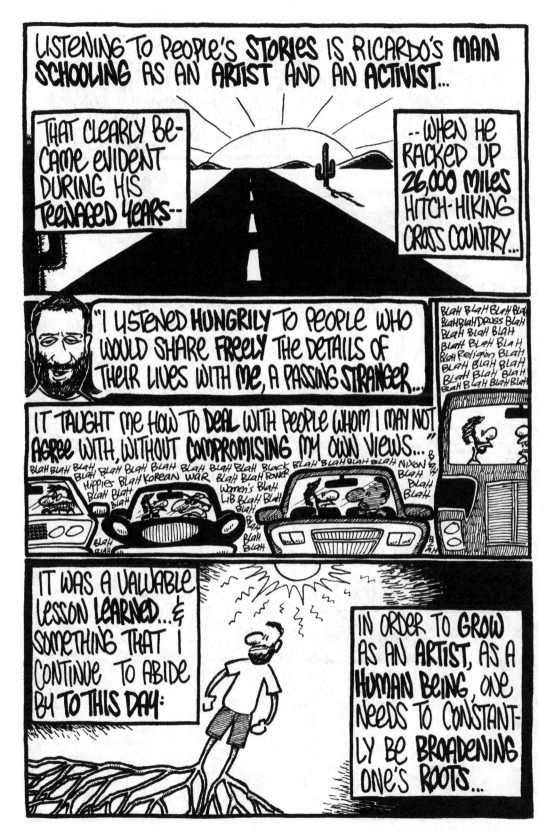

Art by Keith Knight, copyright 2005

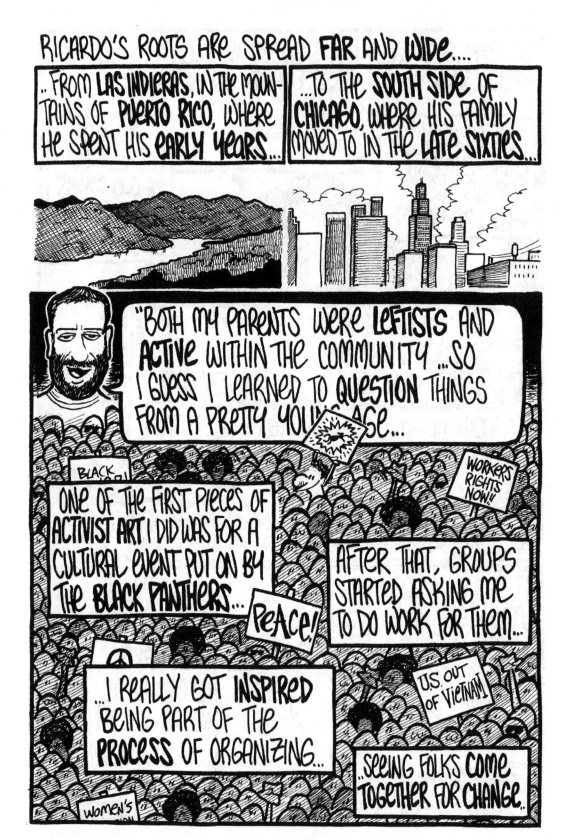

Art by Keith Knight, copyright 2005

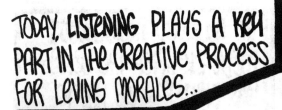

TODAY, LISTENING PLAYS A KEY PART IN THE CREATIVE PROCESS FOR LEVINS MORALES...

Whenever I enter into a new project, I listen & try to assess the situation by asking:

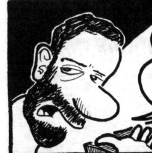

What is the underlying story here? How can a particular image impact that story?

IT IS ALL PART OF THE **VISUAL GRIOT** APPROACH HE TAKES TO HIS ART...

PETER RACHLEFF IS A **LABOR HISTORIAN**.. HE FIRST MET RICARDO FOLLOWING A LOCAL LABOR STRIKE BACK IN 1985..

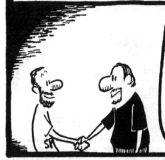

Ricardo & I collaborated on a series of local Labor History articles for a newspaper called The Union Advocate....

IT WAS GREAT TO WORK WITH HIM BECAUSE WE **BOTH** BELIEVE THAT THE **CREATIVE PROCESS** IS JUST AS **VITAL** & **IMPORTANT** AS THE **OUTCOME**.

...THROUGH **RESEARCH** & **INPUT** FROM THE **COMMUNITY**, IMAGES BEGAN TO EMERGE FROM RICARDO'S **PEN**..

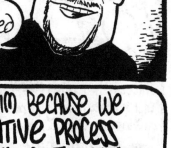

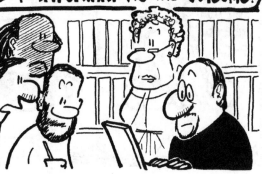

Art by Keith Knight, copyright 2005

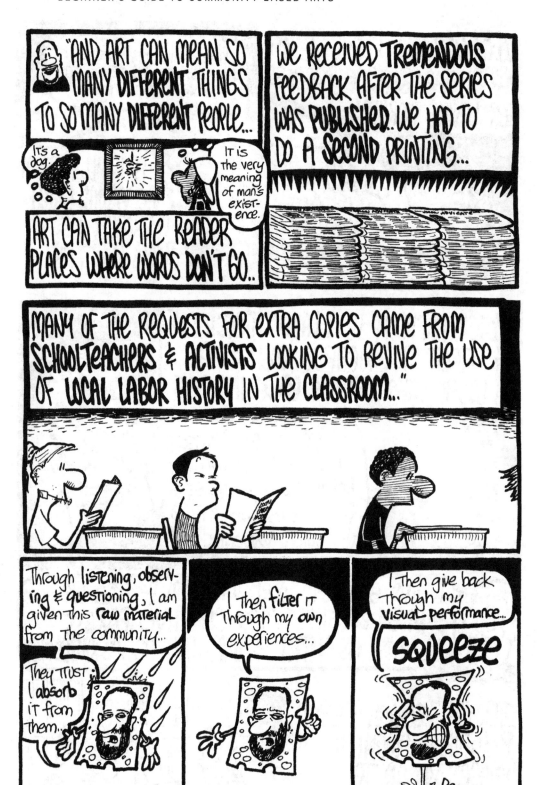

Art by Keith Knight, copyright 2005

MANY OF RICARDO'S PERFORMANCES CAN BE FOUND AT NORTHLAND'S WORKSPACE...

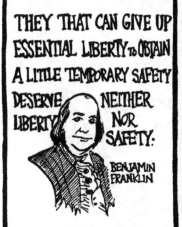

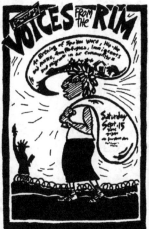

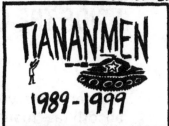

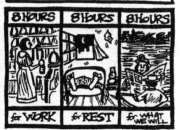

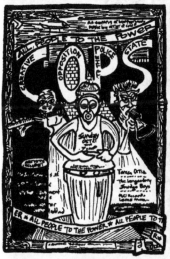

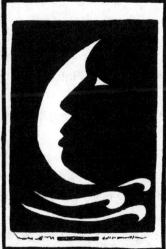

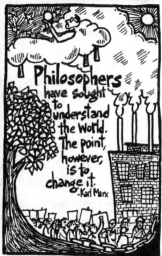

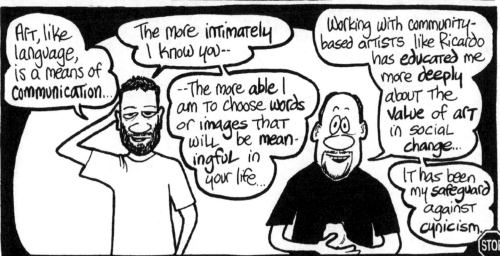

Art by Keith Knight, copyright 2005

INSIDE THE CRAFT CIRCLE

TIP

Listen, observe, question, absorb raw material from the community, filter it through your own experiences and then give it back.

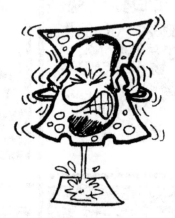

TOPICS

- How can you gather and record information about your community?
- What archives and databases are available to help you get started?
- What listening skills should you develop as you talk with people in your community?
- What are some of the key events in labor history where you live?
- What stories and images do you "soak up" every day?
- When is an image more powerful than words?

TECHNIQUE: COMMUNITY SOUNDING

Derived from exercises of the East Bay Institute for Urban Arts, Oakland, CA

DURATION
Minimum 3 hours (or much longer, in several meetings)

OBJECTIVES
- Art: Gather ideas and content for artistic products.
- Learning: Expand understanding of the chosen theme, and develop listening skills.
- Social Change: Develop community research skills.

MATERIALS
- Pens, pencils, paper, and clipboards
- Xeroxed questions and a local map for engaging people of the community
- Video cameras, still cameras and/or audio recorders for documentation (optional)

IN ADVANCE
- Conduct group discussions to form a consensus about a community theme or issue to be the focus of the work.
- Use databases and archives to research the theme or issue.
- Develop a list of interview questions and listening/observing tasks related to the chosen theme or issue.
- Practice/role-play observing, listening, interviewing, and recording.
- Identify one or more community sites where people with knowledge and opinions are likely to congregate. For example, transit hubs, public buildings, commercial centers, hotels, and theaters.

STEPS
1. On the agreed-upon day and time for the sounding, gather near a community site, split into groups of two or three, and get to work listening, observing, and interviewing.
2. Ask each participant to record and bring back some combination of at least 10 of the following: meaningful phrases, gestures, and snapshots or sketches.

CONTINUED

VARIATIONS / FOLLOW-UP
- Organize a sharing session following the sounding.
  (If there's too much material, have small groups do initial sifting.)
- Discuss which of the gathered signs, symbols, rituals, and stories appear to be common to many people in the community, and how they might be used in a project.
- Observe/listen/interview people on a bus or train instead of at a fixed site.
- Use disposable or cell phone cameras as an alternative for documentation.

In the next story, we go to the region known as

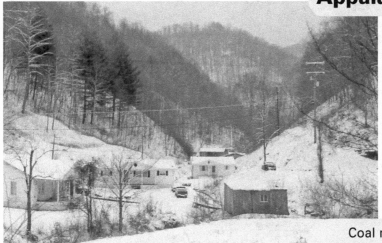

Appalachia and the mountainous states of Kentucky and West Virginia.

Coal mined from beneath these mountaintops generates more than 25% of the nation's electricity...

(2.8 million tons of coal per year).

But the sparks out here are more than just electrical.

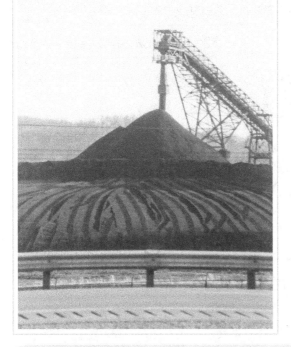

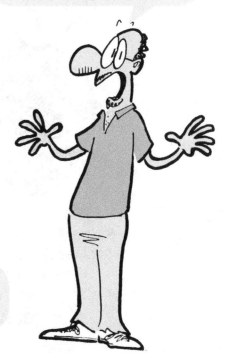

It seems a whole lot of people are steamed up about the dangers of hauling coal across the states' roads and highways.

Parents, truckers, legislators, police, community activists, neighbors are all upset – and each group names the others as the source of the problem.

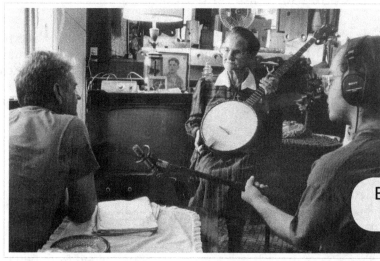

Enter **Tom Hansell...**

...a local man with a lot of questions and not a lot of the answers. His curiosity and determination took him all the way from 12 million years in the past to the man who lives next door.

In the process, he learned an important lesson about how to listen to diverse viewpoints.

One side note:

Kentucky and West Virginia are home to bluegrass and old-time mountain music, so in keeping with the local flavor, we decided to end Tom's story a little differently.

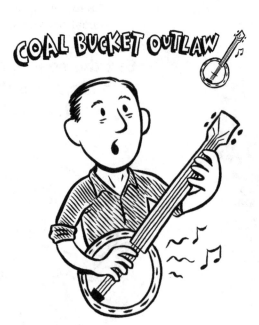

Sit back, listen for the banjo, and consider all the angles to a mighty complex situation we call

"Coal Bucket Outlaw!"

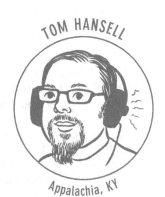

TOM HANSELL

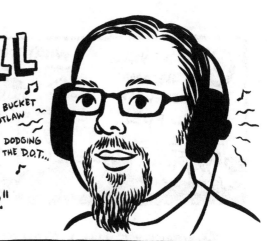

IS A DOCUMENTARY ARTIST AND STORYTELLER WHO LIVES IN WHITESBURG, KENTUCKY, AND WORKS OUT OF AN ORGANIZATION THERE KNOWN AS "APPALSHOP."

COAL BUCKET OUTLAW ~~

DODGING THE D.O.T...

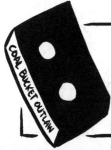

COAL BUCKET OUTLAW

ONE OF TOM'S BEST-KNOWN PROJECTS IS "COAL BUCKET OUTLAW," A DOCUMENTARY SERIES ABOUT COAL-HAULING TRUCKERS IN APPALACHIA.

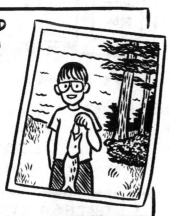

"IT ALL STARTED ON MY 9TH BIRTHDAY, WHEN MY PARENTS TOOK ME CAMPING AND FISHING IN THE MOUNTAINS OF WEST VIRGINIA.

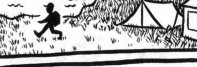

ONE MORNING, I WENT EXPLORING TO FIND ARROWHEADS & FOSSILS.

I WAS INTO FOSSILS. THEY SEEMED MYSTERIOUS, MYSTICAL -- A CONNECTION TO DINOSAURS THAT ROAMED THE EARTH LONG BEFORE HUMANS.

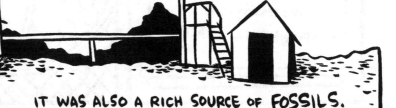

I FOUND AN OLD COAL MINE WITH ALL THE BUILDINGS STILL STANDING...

...AND A HUGE COAL SLAG HEAP IN THE MIDDLE.

I WAS FASCINATED BY HOW BEAUTIFUL AND HOW DISGUSTING IT WAS.

IT WAS ALSO A RICH SOURCE OF FOSSILS.

Art by Ellen Forney, copyright 2005

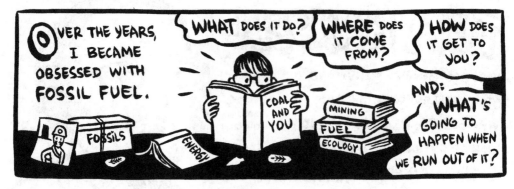

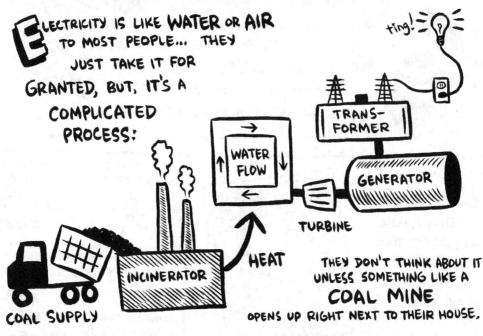

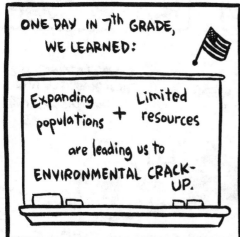

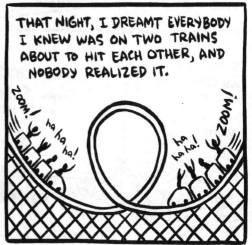

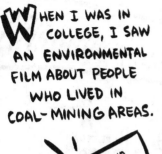

When I was in college, I saw an environmental film about people who lived in coal-mining areas.

On Our Own Land — ADMIT ONE

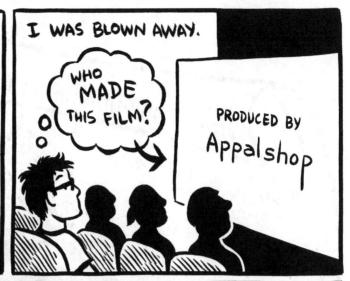

I WAS BLOWN AWAY.

WHO MADE THIS FILM?

PRODUCED BY Appalshop

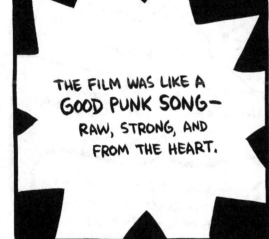

THE FILM WAS LIKE A GOOD PUNK SONG— RAW, STRONG, AND FROM THE HEART.

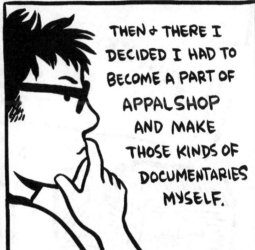

THEN & THERE I DECIDED I HAD TO BECOME A PART OF APPALSHOP AND MAKE THOSE KINDS OF DOCUMENTARIES MYSELF.

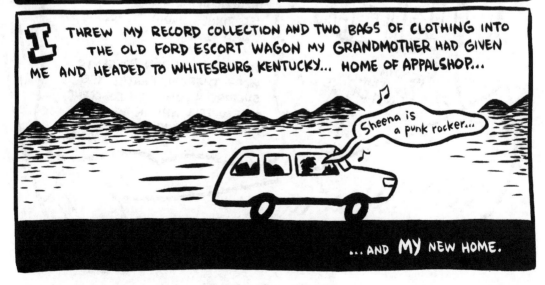

I THREW MY RECORD COLLECTION AND TWO BAGS OF CLOTHING INTO THE OLD FORD ESCORT WAGON MY GRANDMOTHER HAD GIVEN ME AND HEADED TO WHITESBURG, KENTUCKY... HOME OF APPALSHOP...

Sheena is a punk rocker...

...AND MY NEW HOME.

Art by Ellen Forney, copyright 2005

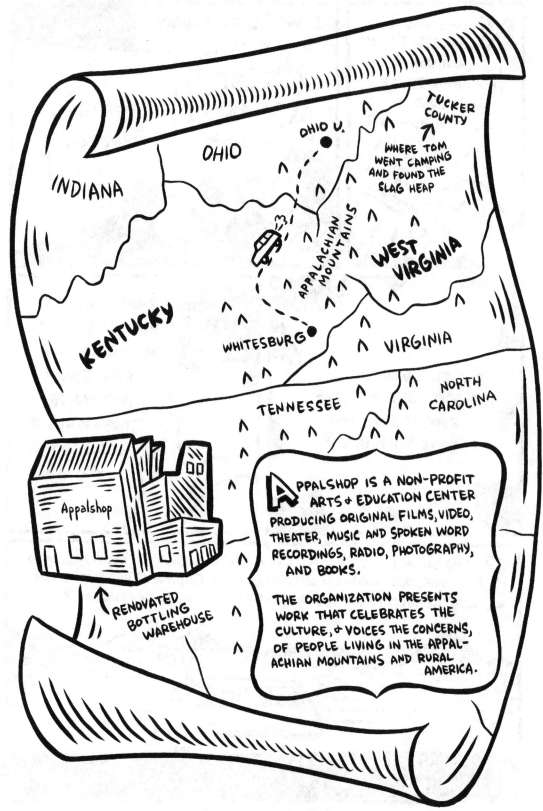

Art by Ellen Forney, copyright 2005

AFTER YEARS OF PRODUCTION WORK AS AN ASSISTANT AT APPALSHOP, I DECIDED ON COAL-HAULING TRUCKERS AS MY FOCUS.

WITHOUT THE TRUCK DRIVERS WHO HAUL COAL FROM THE MINES TO THE PROCESSING PLANTS, MILLIONS OF PEOPLE WOULD BE WITHOUT ELECTRICITY.

BUT, IN ORDER TO MAKE A LIVING, MANY OF THE MEN WHO DRIVE THESE "COAL BUCKETS" HAVE TO HAUL MUCH MORE THAN THE SAFE & LEGAL WEIGHT LIMIT...

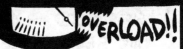

OVERLOAD!!

... WHICH HAS LED TO THE DEATHS OF BOTH TRUCKERS AND PEOPLE WHO LIVE OR DRIVE ON COAL-HAULING ROADWAYS.

IT'S A SERIOUS AND GROWING PROBLEM WITH THE DIFFERENT VIEWPOINTS THAT **SOMEHOW** NEED TO COME TOGETHER.

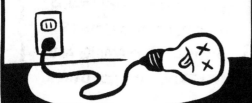

MY SOLUTION WAS TO HOOK UP WITH MY NEIGHBOR **HERBIE ADAMS**, A COAL-HAULING TRUCKER.

HOP IN, PAL!

↑ 4 AM!

ENTUC

SITTING IN THE PASSENGER SEAT WASN'T VERY EXCITING, BUT I LEARNED HOW TRUCKING TAKES **NERVES OF STEEL** AND A SHARP EYE.

YOU MISJUDGE THE SPEED OR DIRECTION OF YOUR VEHICLE BY EVEN AN INCH AND IT COULD COST NOT ONLY TENS OF THOUSANDS OF DOLLARS... BUT **LIVES**.

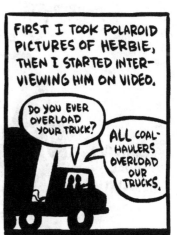

FIRST I TOOK POLAROID PICTURES OF HERBIE, THEN I STARTED INTERVIEWING HIM ON VIDEO.

DO YOU EVER OVERLOAD YOUR TRUCK?

ALL COAL-HAULERS OVERLOAD OUR TRUCKS.

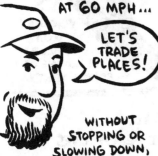

ONE DAY, WHILE DRIVING DOWN A MOUNTAIN AT 60 MPH...

LET'S TRADE PLACES!

WITHOUT STOPPING OR SLOWING DOWN, I SLID OVER INTO HIS SEAT.

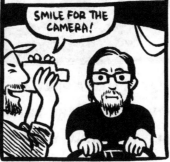

HE GAVE ME STEP-BY-STEP INSTRUCTIONS ON HOW TO DRIVE THE TRUCK.

SMILE FOR THE CAMERA!

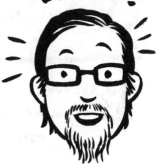

THERE I WAS... A COAL BUCKET OUTLAW!

Art by Ellen Forney, copyright 2005

AFTER THAT INITIAL INTERVIEW, IT BECAME EASIER TO GET PEOPLE TO TALK... I WAS OFF AND RUNNING.

HOLLYWOOD FILMS TELL STORIES AS IF THERE ARE ONLY **TWO** SIDES: **GOOD** AND **BAD.** THIS **SELLS TICKETS,** BUT IT DOESN'T HELP **CHANGE** ANYTHING.

A HEALTHY COMMUNITY HAS SPACES WHERE PEOPLE CAN TALK OPENLY ABOUT THEIR DIFFERENT VIEWPOINTS WITHOUT SCREAMING AND HOLLERING AT EACH OTHER.

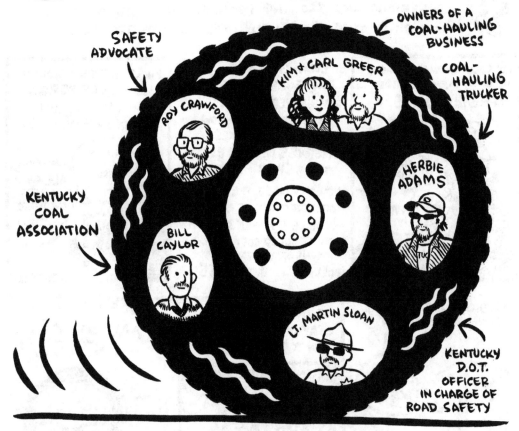

SAFETY ADVOCATE

ROY CRAWFORD

KIM & CARL GREER

OWNERS OF A COAL-HAULING BUSINESS

COAL-HAULING TRUCKER

HERBIE ADAMS

KENTUCKY COAL ASSOCIATION

BILL CAYLOR

LT. MARTIN SLOAN

KENTUCKY D.O.T. OFFICER IN CHARGE OF ROAD SAFETY

EVERYONE'S VIEWPOINT IS LIKE A PART OF A WHEEL... ONLY BY LISTENING TO ALL THE DIFFERENT PERSPECTIVES CAN YOU GET THE WHOLE WHEEL ROLLING.

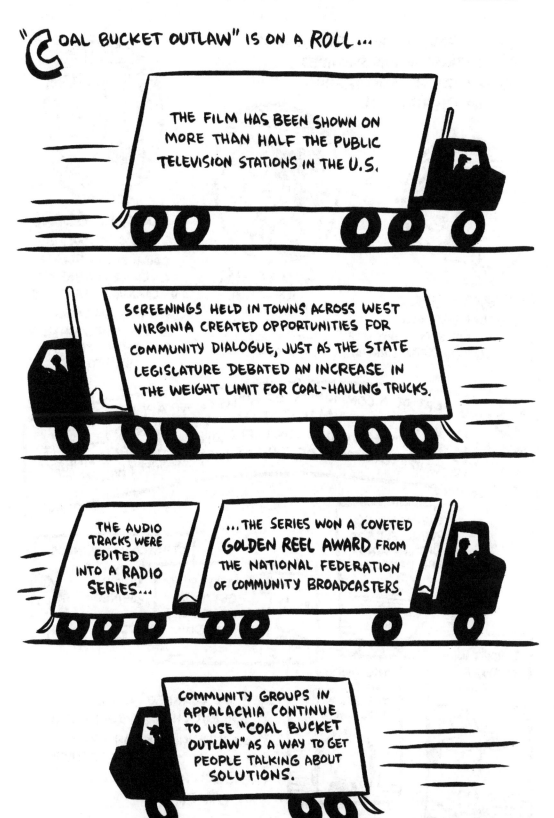

Art by Ellen Forney, copyright 2005

ALL ALONG THE WAY, EVERYONE AT APPALSHOP HAS PROVIDED SOME SORT OF MENTORSHIP OR INSPIRATION...

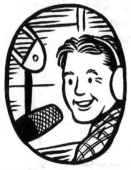

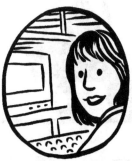

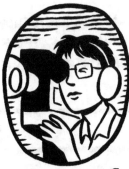

ELIZABETH BARRET, A GREAT FILMMAKER, IS ONE OF THE MOST HOSPITABLE AND **WELCOMING** PEOPLE I KNOW.

ANN LEWIS, FILM EDITOR, TAUGHT ME ABOUT INVOLVING COMMUNITY GROUPS DIRECTLY IN PRODUCTION.

BUCK MAGGARD, RADIO PRODUCER, COULD REALLY RELATE TO PEOPLE IN A VARIETY OF COMMUNITY SETTINGS. HE WAS ESPECIALLY GOOD AT USING **HUMOR** TO DIFFUSE STRESSFUL SITUATIONS.

BEING PART OF A COMMUNITY OF ARTISTS AT APPALSHOP HAS DEFINED MY WORK AND MY **VALUES**. I LEARNED HOW TO **RESPECT** FOLKS, REALLY **LISTEN** TO THEM, AND TO DEAL WITH PEOPLE AS **PEOPLE** RATHER THAN JUST REPRESENTATIVES OF THIS OR THAT PERSPECTIVE.

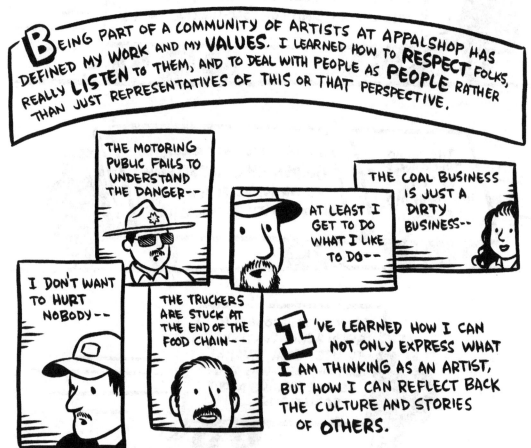

THE MOTORING PUBLIC FAILS TO UNDERSTAND THE DANGER--

AT LEAST I GET TO DO WHAT I LIKE TO DO--

THE COAL BUSINESS IS JUST A DIRTY BUSINESS--

I DON'T WANT TO HURT NOBODY--

THE TRUCKERS ARE STUCK AT THE END OF THE FOOD CHAIN--

I'VE LEARNED HOW I CAN NOT ONLY EXPRESS WHAT I AM THINKING AS AN ARTIST, BUT HOW I CAN REFLECT BACK THE CULTURE AND STORIES OF **OTHERS**.

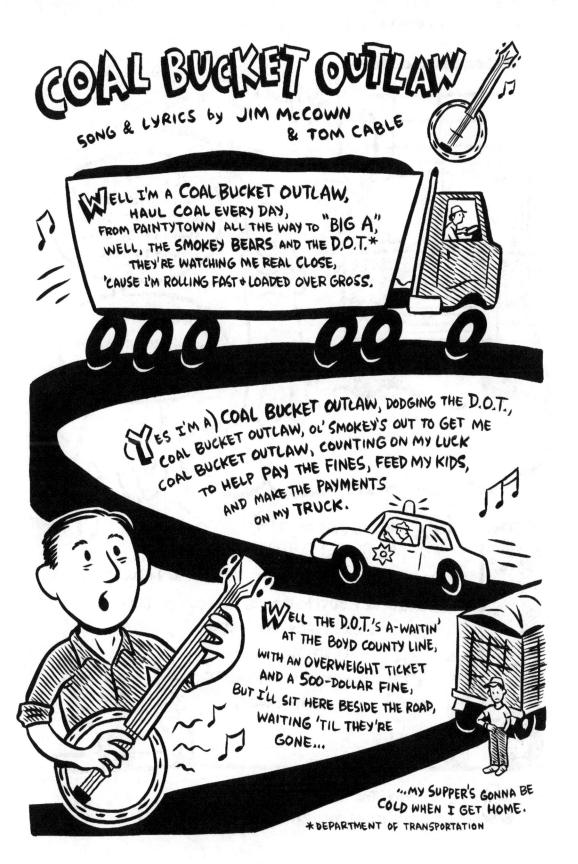

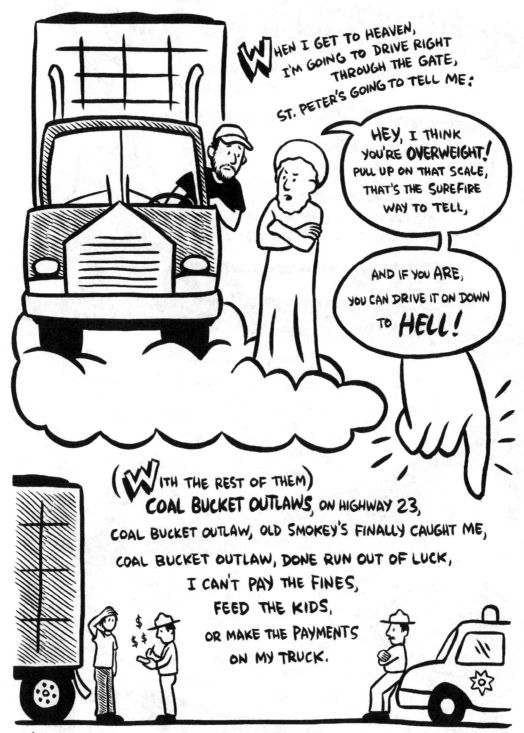

Art by Ellen Forney, copyright 2005

INSIDE THE CRAFT CIRCLE

TIP

Everyone's viewpoint is like part of a wheel. Only by listening to all the different perspectives can you get the whole wheel rolling.

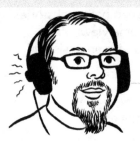

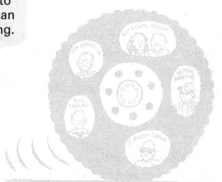

TOPICS

- We depend on electricity, but the systems for generating and delivering it are almost invisible. What other invisible systems are important in your community?
- What types of people are on the "spokes" of those systems?
- What will every person on the wheel generally agree upon? Where are they likely to disagree?
- What does it take to portray a viewpoint that you don't agree with?

TECHNIQUE: STORY CIRCLES

Derived from exercises of the Roadside Theater, a division of Appalshop, Whitesburg, KY

DURATION

1 hour to 1 day

OBJECTIVES

- Art: Develop listening and verbal expression skills.
- Learning: Understand the relationship between personal stories and social issues, and develop tolerance for diverse viewpoints.
- Social Change: Gather anecdotal information for analysis and community education.

MATERIALS

No materials are essential, but it's helpful to have:

- Comfortable, movable chairs for participants
- A relatively quiet, private space (however, story circles have been held in gymnasiums with hundreds of people)

IN ADVANCE

- In group discussions, agree upon a theme related to an invisible system in your community, that supports the group's purpose. For example: water, transportation, sewage treatment, garbage disposal, food production, criminal justice, social service networks.
- Choose a facilitator who can explain the purpose of the gathering, and be responsible for beginning, moving along, and closing the circle(s).
- It is important for the facilitator be aware of diverse viewpoints about the issue.

STEPS

1. Gather in one or more circles of 5 to 15 people, facing each other.

2. Begin with a story or explanation that sets the tone for the purpose and theme of the circle(s). Ask who in the circle(s) has a related story to tell.

3. Go around the circle(s), with each person in turn either telling a story or passing.

4. Before ending, ask if people who have passed would now like to speak.

5. Reflect on what differing viewpoints emerged from the circle.

6. When possible, end with a poem or song (perhaps led by a participant) that brings closure to the spirit of the particular gathering.

7. Leave time for participants to talk informally afterwards.

NOTES

- Discourage participants from thinking too much about what they will say when it is their turn. Spontaneity is important.
- Before beginning the circle, explain to participants that they must not have side conversations, make comments, or ask the storyteller questions.

ACTION

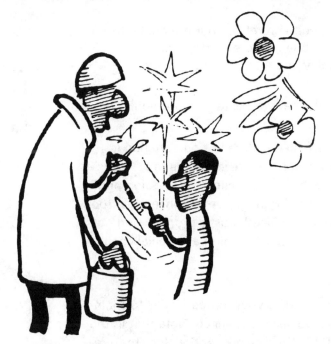

Produce a new work of art that
positively impacts the community.

Action is where your investigations transition into producing one or more new works of art.

The group must blend its many perspectives, abilities, ideas and emotions into a unified whole, so that new creative products can inform and move others. Action is where the artistic rubber hits the community road:

Bring together the various kinds of information, ideas and images you have gathered.

Shape, edit and **refine** your material into one or more works of art (play, mural, film, concerto, etc.).

Present the new works to the community.

In a product-oriented culture like ours, Action is often the artistic territory that receives the most focus – sometimes too much. As the excitement of going public builds, it will be easy for the group to concentrate too much energy on the finished artistic product, and not enough on the processes of learning and social change.

This makes your job as leader to maintain a sense of balance. Note that in the CRAFT framework, **Action** (i.e. the creation of a product) is neither the beginning nor the end, but the middle.

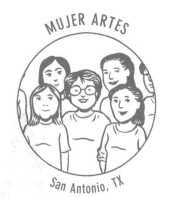

MUJER ARTES

San Antonio, TX

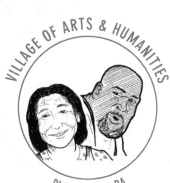

VILLAGE OF ARTS & HUMANITIES

Philadelphia, PA

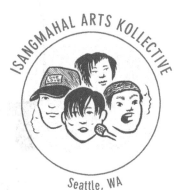

ISANGMAHAL ARTS KOLLECTIVE

Seattle, WA

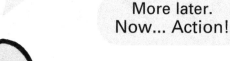

More later.
Now... Action!

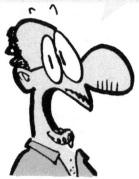

We are on our way to **San Antonio, Texas,** the 8th largest city in the nation.

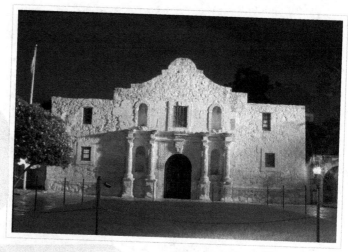

This city has had a rough and tumble history ever since the Spaniards forcibly built a mission, later known as the Alamo, here on the site of a Coahuiltecan Indian village.

Over time, competing indian tribes, the Spanish military, Catholic missionaries, colonists and settlers – some with African slaves - carved a bumpy coexistence.

Unfortunately, one incident has eclipsed the city's long history. Thanks to books, movies, and souvenirs, most everyone in America knows the slogan: "Remember the Alamo!"

Well, the siege of the Alamo is a dramatic story, but it has become the focal point of long standing tensions between different community groups.

Today it is the descendants of those who first inhabited the land who are most likely to be underhoused, undernourished and underemployed. Residents of indigenous and Mexican descent are three times more likely to live in poverty, with women and senior citizens facing the toughest circumstances.

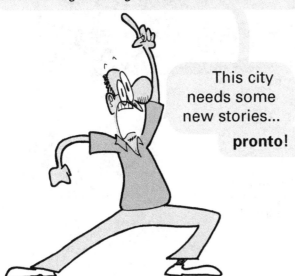

This city needs some new stories... **pronto!**

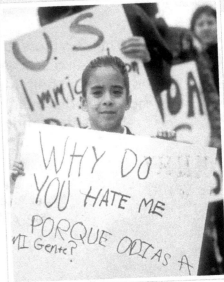

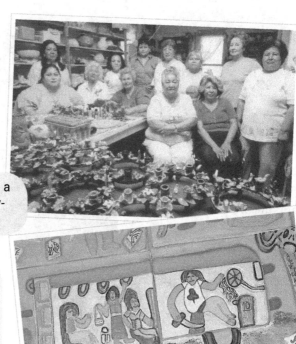

Luckily for San Antonio, there is a sort of story factory over on the west side of town.

Most every day, six hours a day, an unusual team of story-tellers is here hard at work....

They are manufacturing a new mythology using a powerful combination of ceramics and coop-eration. Their bowls, vases, cups and sculptures tell little-known stories unearthed from the community.

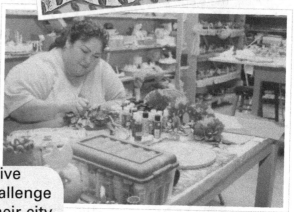

This group takes Action as only art-ists can – they tell the stories others don't or won't, the stories too deeply buried for polite conversation or too controversial for the mass media.

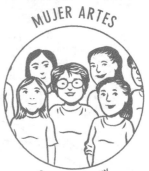

Their bold creative expressions directly challenge stereotypes and help their city reclaim, rediscover and redefine its identity.

These are the women of **Mujer Artes**. We call their story **"Comadres."**

MUJER ARTES

San Antonio, TX

~ MUJER ARTES ~

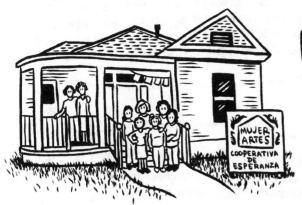

MUJER ARTES IS A WOMEN'S POTTERY COLLECTIVE BASED IN SAN ANTONIO, TEXAS. MUJER ARTES ("WOMAN ARTS") IS MADE UP OF EIGHTEEN WOMEN AGES 37 TO 73 WHO MEET TO CREATE POTTERY DRAWN FROM ASPECTS OF THEIR CULTURE AND COMMUNITY.

MOST HOMES IN SAN ANTONIO ARE NO DIFFERENT FROM ANYWHERE ELSE IN THE U.S., BARRAGED WITH STEREOTYPED IMAGES OF MEXICAN AMERICANS IN THE NEWSPAPERS, TELEVISION, AND MOVIES.

same ol' stereotype →

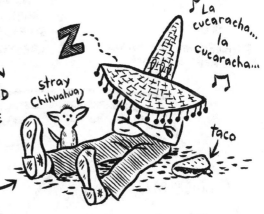

Stray Chihuahua

♪ La cucaracha... la cucaracha... ♪

taco

BUT FROM INSIDE A MODEST OLD HOUSE IN THE HEART OF THE WESTSIDE NEIGHBORHOOD, MUJER ARTES IS CREATING AN ALTERNATIVE.

PAPER CUTOUTS HANG THROUGHOUT THE SPACE, TENS OF SHELVES ARE CHOCK FULL OF CERAMICS OF ALL SIZES, SHAPES, AND COLORS: SOME FEATURE ANCIENT ICONOGRAPHY, OTHERS CONTAIN FUNNY, CONTROVERSIAL IMAGES OF TODAY.

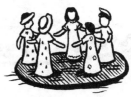

SOME ARE TIMELESS.

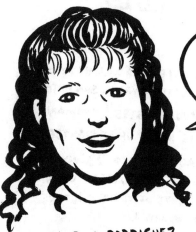

CYNTHIA RODRIGUEZ
Mujer Artes Studio
Coordinator

Born: 1968

Former Customer Service
Representative

WE COME FROM ALL AGES AND WORK BACK-GROUNDS. WE SPEAK OUT AS MEXICANOS FOR OUR HERITAGE AND TO ENCOURAGE PEOPLE TO REMEMBER THEIR CULTURE AND HISTORY.

EVERY WOMAN COMES TO MUJER ARTES FOR HER OWN REASONS, BUT TOGETHER WE BECOME SOMETHING MUCH, MUCH BIGGER...

WE HAVE CREATED A TRULY JOINT VENTURE WHERE THE IMPORTANCE OF TELLING OUR STORIES AND THE STORIES OF OUR COMMUNITY ARE THE GLUE THAT HOLDS US TOGETHER.

EACH WOMAN MAKES A MONTHLY STIPEND PLUS A PERCENTAGE OF THE SALES OF OUR INDIVIDUAL AND COOPERATIVE PIECES.

MOST DAYS, WE WORK COOPERATIVELY, BUT ONE DAY EACH WEEK WE DO OUR INDIVIDUAL WORK. WE TALK, WE ARGUE, WE SHARE IDEAS, AND WE BUILD COMMUNITY. WE ARE LIKE comadres.*

* comadre
SPANISH: "co-mother, the godmother."
It also means "comrade," "sister," "soulmate"... a special friendship.

Art by Ellen Forney, copyright 2005

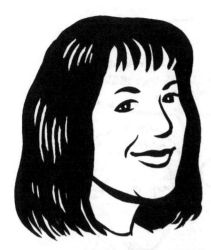

IMELDA ARISMENDEZ
Born: 1949
Campus Minister

AT MUJER ARTES, CHANGE HAPPENS AT DIFFERENT LEVELS: INDIVIDUAL, GROUP, AND COMMUNITY, EACH DAY, un poquito ["A LITTLE BIT"].

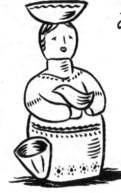

La Peru
by Imelda Arismendez

INSPIRED BY IMELDA'S VISIT TO PERU. "PERUVIAN WOMEN ARE SO RESOURCEFUL. THEY SHOULD BE AN INSPIRATION TO US IN THE U.S."

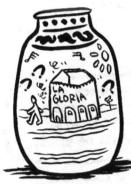

La Gloria by Carmen Medrano

"NEIGHBORS ORGANIZED TO HELP SAVE A BELOVED SAN ANTONIO THEATER FROM THE WRECKING BALL."

WE SHARE IDEAS AND TECHNIQUES. WE SHARE STORIES. WE GET TO COMPARE OUR EXPERIENCES — BOTH THE GOOD ONES AND THE BAD ONES — AND DECIDE FOR OURSELVES WHAT WE BELIEVE IN.

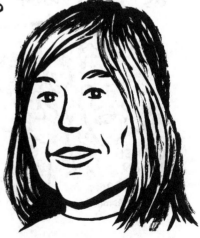

CARMEN MEDRANO
Born: 1951
Former factory worker

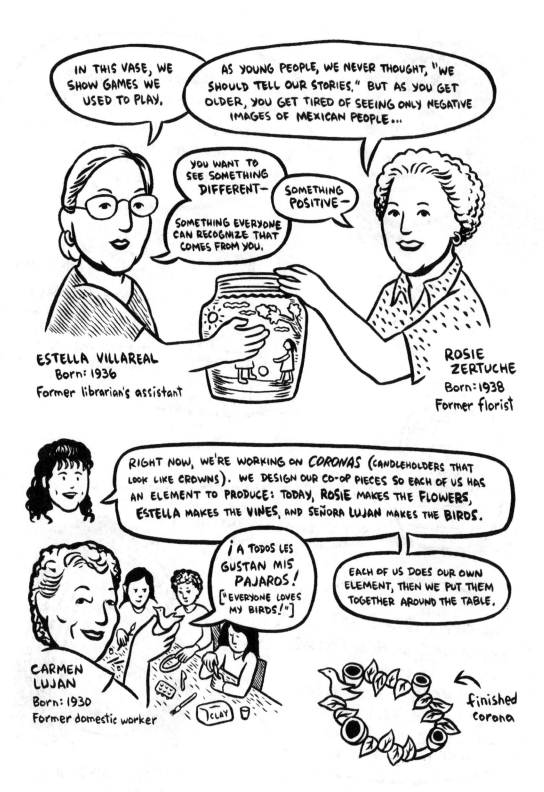

MUJER ARTES TELL THEIR OWN STORIES AND THE STORIES OF OTHER WOMEN FROM AROUND THE WORLD...

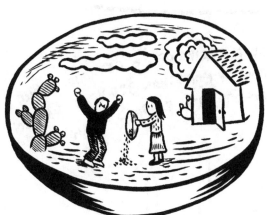

La Peleya de los Frijoles
["THE HAIRY BEANS INCIDENT"]
By Imelda Arismendez

"THIS POT COMMEMORATES THE TIME WE MUJER ARTES HAD A BIG FIGHT OVER WHO WAS GOING TO CLEAN THE REFRIGERATOR!"

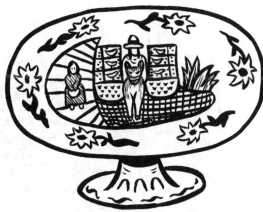

Pajarero
["THE BIRDSELLER"]
By Carmen Lujan

"THIS CAKE PLATE HAS AN EVERY-DAY IMAGE FROM RURAL MEXICO OF THE 1940'S. IT'S MY WAY TO REMIND PEOPLE OF OUR ROOTS."

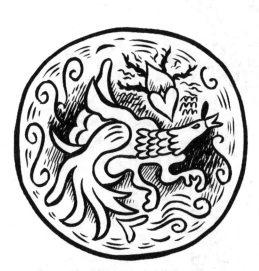

La Rayona
["THE FEMALE ROOSTER"]
By Cynthia Rodriguez

"THIS PLATE TELLS A JOKE ABOUT HOW I AM THE 'BIG BOSS' OF MUJER ARTES."

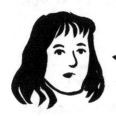

WE ALSO SPEAK OUT ON THE ISSUES FACING US AS MEXICANS, AMERICANS, AND WOMEN.

IN 2003, MUJER ARTES PRODUCED A SERIES OF 26 CERAMIC WORKS COMMEMORATING THE BRUTAL DEATHS OF MORE THAN 320 YOUNG WOMEN IN CIUDAD JUAREZ, MEXICO, ON THE BORDER WITH EL PASO, TEXAS.

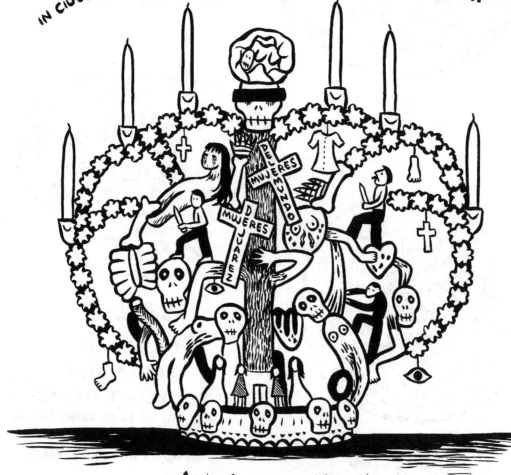

Arbol de la Muerte
["TREE OF DEATH"]
By Veronica Castillo

Art by Ellen Forney, copyright 2005

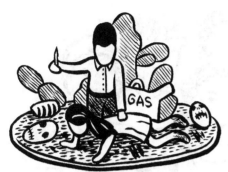

Muerte en Llamas ["DEATH IN FLAMES"]
By Rosa Soria-Peña

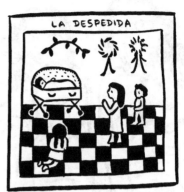

La Despedida ["THE FAREWELL"]
By Lucila Vicencio

Since may of 1993, these young women have been kidnapped, mutilated, raped, and murdered in serial killings — amnesty international has declared them "crimes against humanity," the majority of the victims have been poor, migrant factory workers.

For almost 10 years, the owners of the MAQUILADORAS [BORDER FACTORIES] and the media from both the U.S. and Mexico showed little interest in investigating the deaths.

Thanks to the attention brought to the issue by mujer artes and groups around the world, the murders are finally being recognized and investigated.

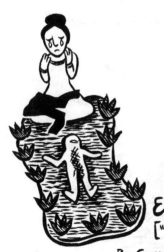

El Vestido ["THE DRESS"]
By Carmen Lujan

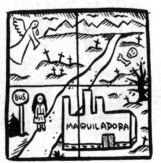

Sueños quebrados ["BROKEN DREAMS"]
By Dee Ann Zertuche Guájardo

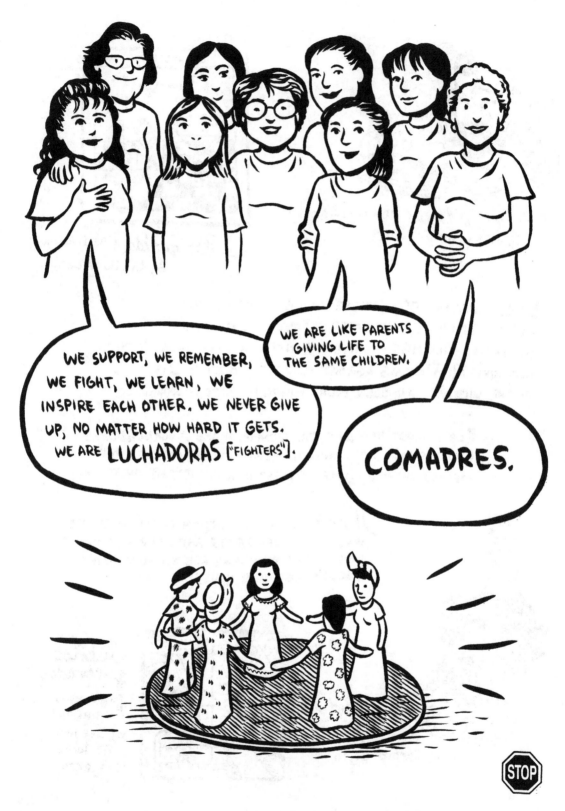

Art by Ellen Forney, copyright 2005

INSIDE THE CRAFT CIRCLE

TIP

Tell the untold stories.

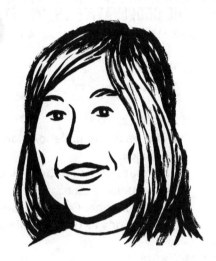

TOPICS

- What stories in your community need to be told?
- How might individual, group, and community stories be told through your artwork?
- Is there a sign, symbol, ritual, or story from your research that could act as a central metaphor?
- Are there opportunities for you to support and expand upon local craft traditions?

TECHNIQUE: LA COOPERATIVA THEMA (THE COOPERATIVE THEME) EXERCISE

Derived from exercises of Mujer Artes, San Antonio, TX

DURATION
Minimum 4 weeks

OBJECTIVES
- Art: In a group collaboration, move from concept to finished art piece.
- Learning: Examine the connections between personal and community issues.
- Social Change: Communicate understanding of these connections to broad audiences.

MATERIALS
- Tape recorder
- Journals, pens
- Large pieces of paper, masking tape, markers
- Quiet room with table(s) and wall space

IN ADVANCE
- Agree upon a common social change theme and begin to research it.

STEPS

Week One: Contact

1. Invite an expert from the community to work with the group. (An expert can be a teacher, activist, elder, or any resident who has experience and knowledge about your theme.)

2. Ask this person to provide three to five key questions to elicit the group's opinions. (The questions from Topics are good examples.)

3. Ask each participant to write their own answers, then share them with the group.

4. Write short phrases on large sheets of paper, to reinforce the most powerful images that come up in this discussion.

Week Two: Research

5. Each participant selects images and stories to research in depth, using films, interviews, newspapers, books, and the internet.

Week Three: Action

6. Compare drafts of the research and share resources. Identify and agree upon a common theme that unites the work.

Week Four: Feedback

7. Continue to refine and compare the work as needed, to meld the pieces into a complete collective work.

VARIATIONS / FOLLOW-UP
- Broaden the scale of the project by working on it over a longer period of time.
- Invite the experts back during the Feedback process to see how the project has evolved.

Next stop is

Philadelphia, Pennsylvania,
population 1.6 million people.

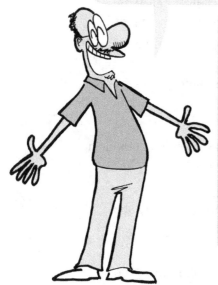

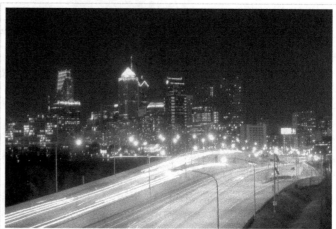

Like many older cities, economic resources here are severely depleted. Most people living in the so-called "inner core" of the city lack the most basic infrastructure – decent schools, adequate housing, safe streets.

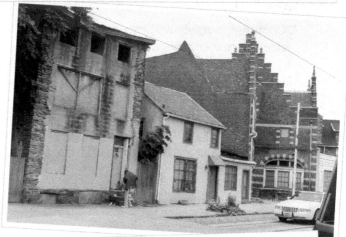

Let's zoom in closer to a ten-square-block area in North Philadelphia, near the neighborhood called

Fairhill.

This is an especially hard-hit neighborhood in a city full of hard-hit neighborhoods...

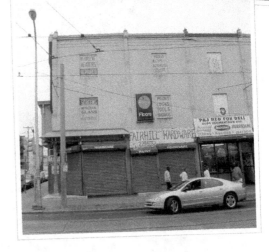

During the 2000 census, 20% of the homes here (one out of every five) were vacant and half of all residents fell below the poverty line, with 41% of households earning less than $10,000. Ten percent of the adults were unemployed, more than two times the national average.

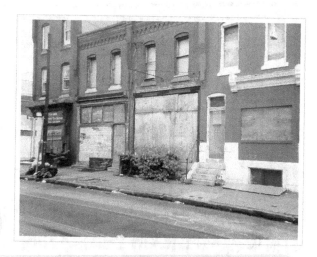

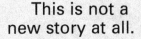
This is not a new story at all.

Normally, people in neighborhoods like this have three choices: (a) accept the circumstances; (b) fight against improvements biased towards bringing in wealthier people; or (c) leave as soon as possible. None of these options is really viable.

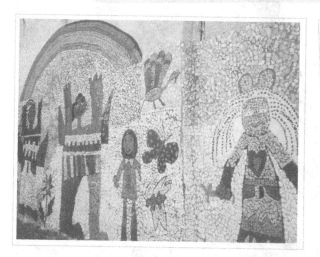

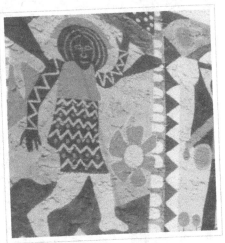

Some people here had a different idea – they decided to "dig in" and rebuild, one vacant property at a time. All it took was an unusual partnership between an artist from across the ocean and a man from up the street, to make things begin to happen.

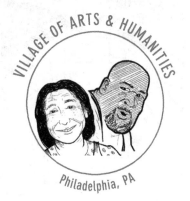

VILLAGE OF ARTS & HUMANITIES

Philadelphia, PA

Meet master mosaic artists **Lily Yeh** and **James Maxton**, just two of the 10,000 individuals who live, work and play within the boundaries of **"That Luminous Place."**

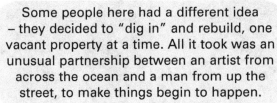

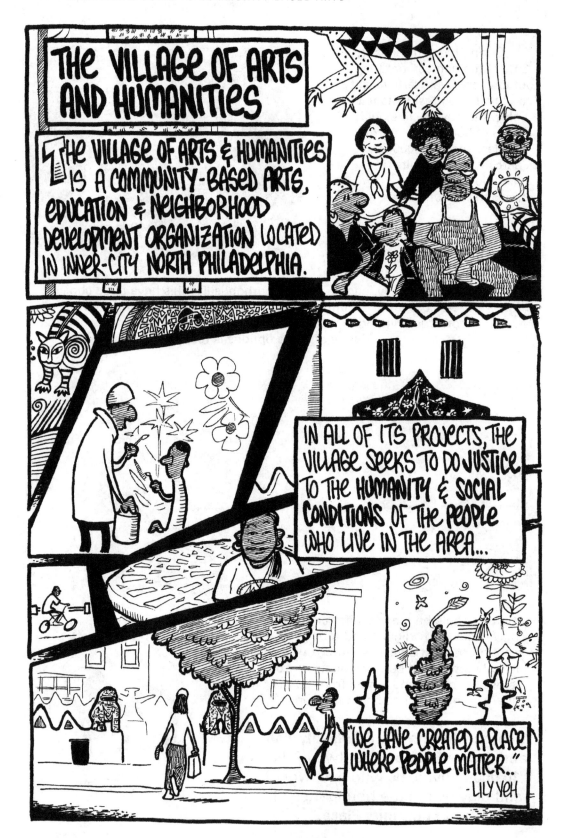

Art by Keith Knight, copyright 2005

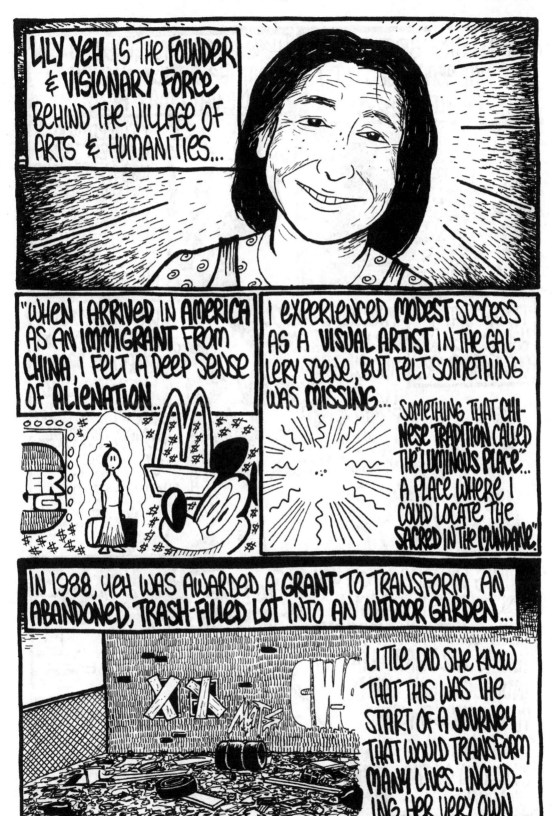

LILY YEH IS THE FOUNDER & VISIONARY FORCE BEHIND THE VILLAGE OF ARTS & HUMANITIES...

"WHEN I ARRIVED IN AMERICA AS AN IMMIGRANT FROM CHINA, I FELT A DEEP SENSE OF ALIENATION...

I EXPERIENCED MODEST SUCCESS AS A VISUAL ARTIST IN THE GALLERY SCENE, BUT FELT SOMETHING WAS MISSING...

SOMETHING THAT CHINESE TRADITION CALLED THE "LUMINOUS PLACE"... A PLACE WHERE I COULD LOCATE THE SACRED IN THE MUNDANE."

IN 1988, YEH WAS AWARDED A GRANT TO TRANSFORM AN ABANDONED, TRASH-FILLED LOT INTO AN OUTDOOR GARDEN...

LITTLE DID SHE KNOW THAT THIS WAS THE START OF A JOURNEY THAT WOULD TRANSFORM MANY LIVES...INCLUDING HER VERY OWN.

Art by Keith Knight, copyright 2005

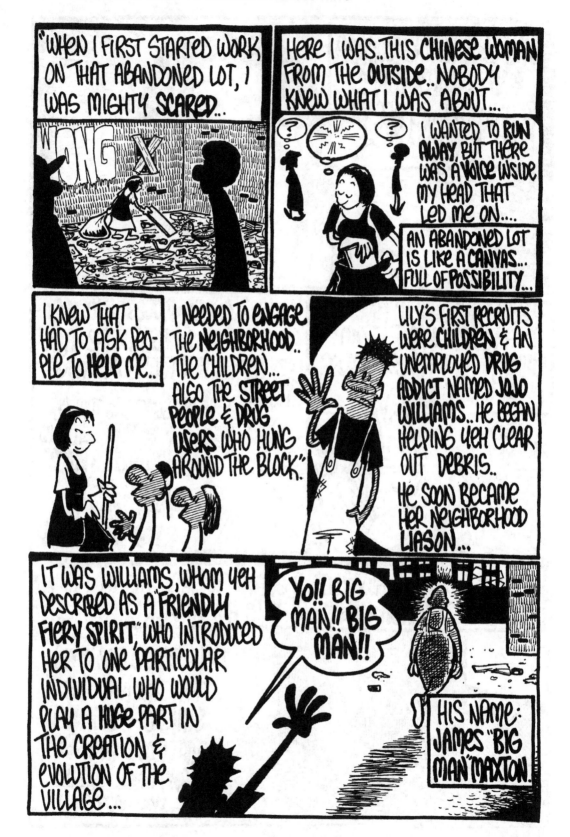

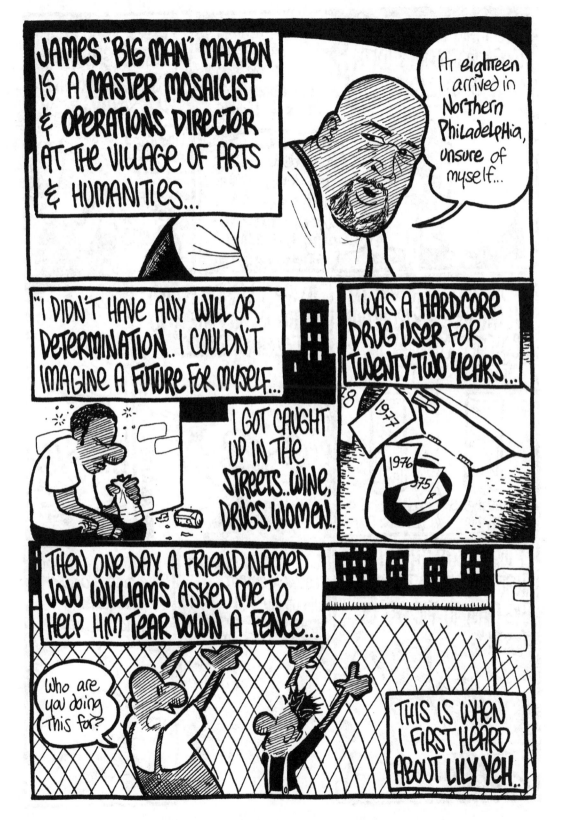

Art by Keith Knight, copyright 2005

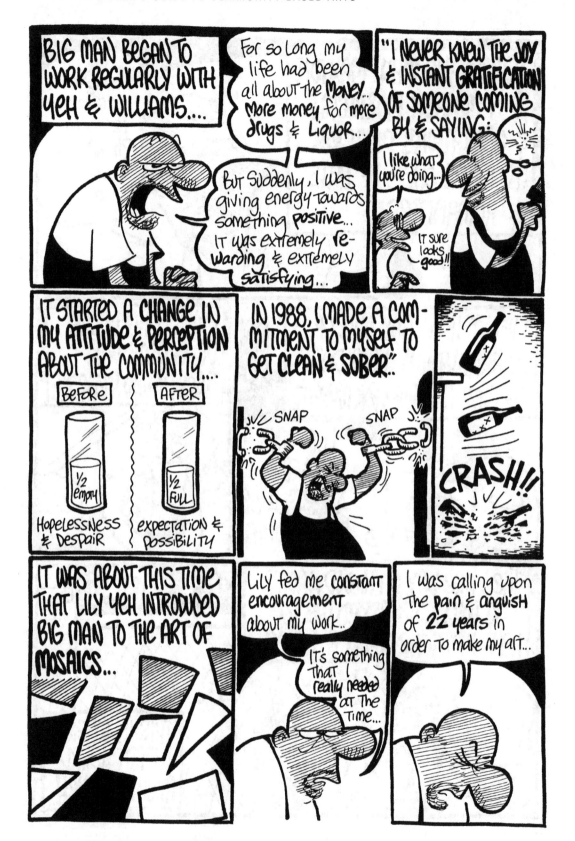

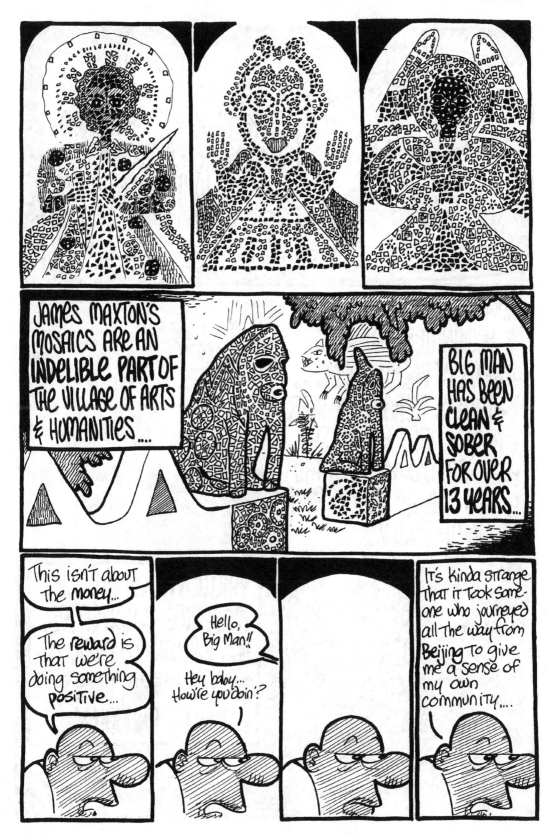

Art by Keith Knight, copyright 2005

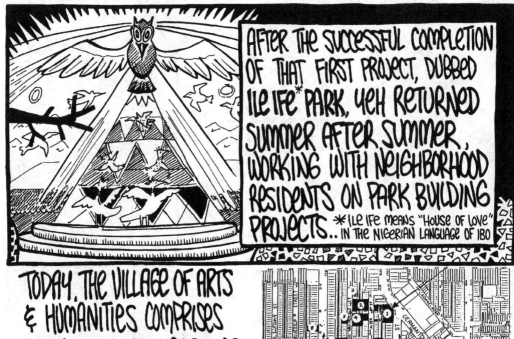

AFTER THE SUCCESSFUL COMPLETION OF THAT FIRST PROJECT, DUBBED ILE IFE* PARK, 4EH RETURNED SUMMER AFTER SUMMER, WORKING WITH NEIGHBORHOOD RESIDENTS ON PARK BUILDING PROJECTS... *ILE IFE MEANS "HOUSE OF LOVE" IN THE NIGERIAN LANGUAGE OF IBO

TODAY, THE VILLAGE OF ARTS & HUMANITIES COMPRISES DOZENS OF PARKS, GARDENS, BUILDINGS, MURALS, CLASSES & EVENTS THAT AFFECT SEVERAL NEIGHBORHOODS WITHIN A 260 SQUARE BLOCK AREA OF NORTH PHILLY...

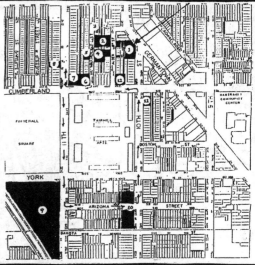

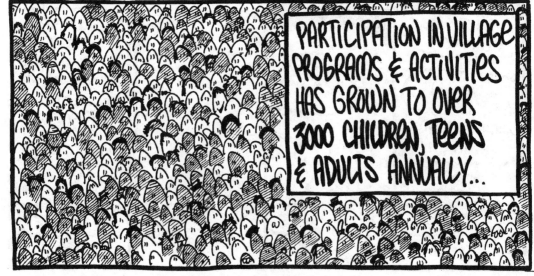

PARTICIPATION IN VILLAGE PROGRAMS & ACTIVITIES HAS GROWN TO OVER 3000 CHILDREN, TEENS & ADULTS ANNUALLY...

Art by Keith Knight, copyright 2005

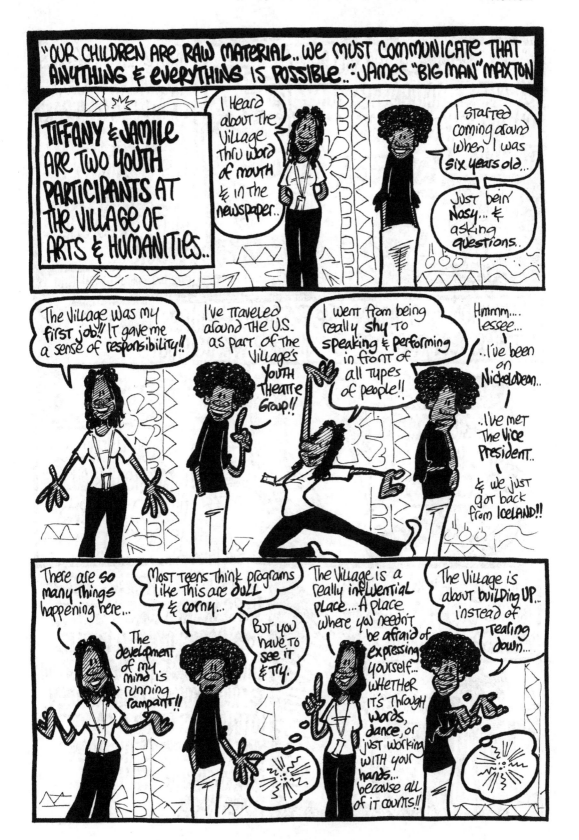

Art by Keith Knight, copyright 2005

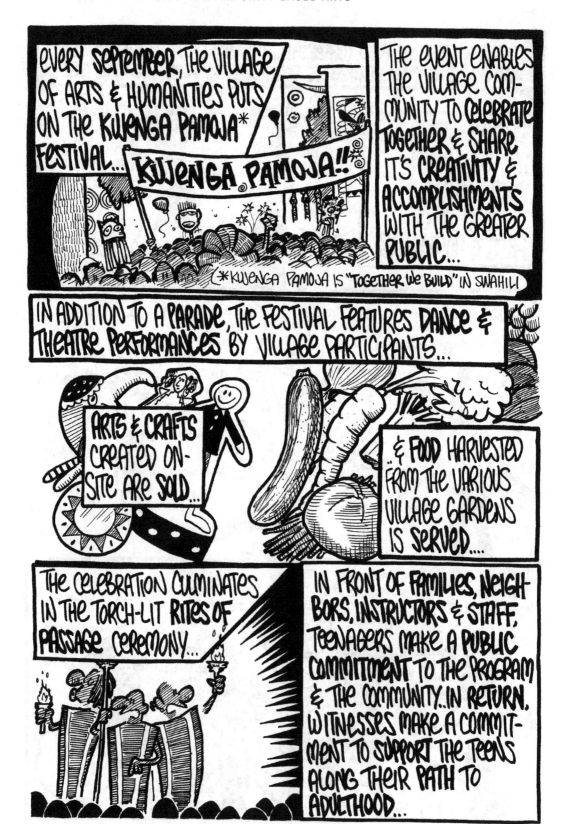

Art by Keith Knight, copyright 2005

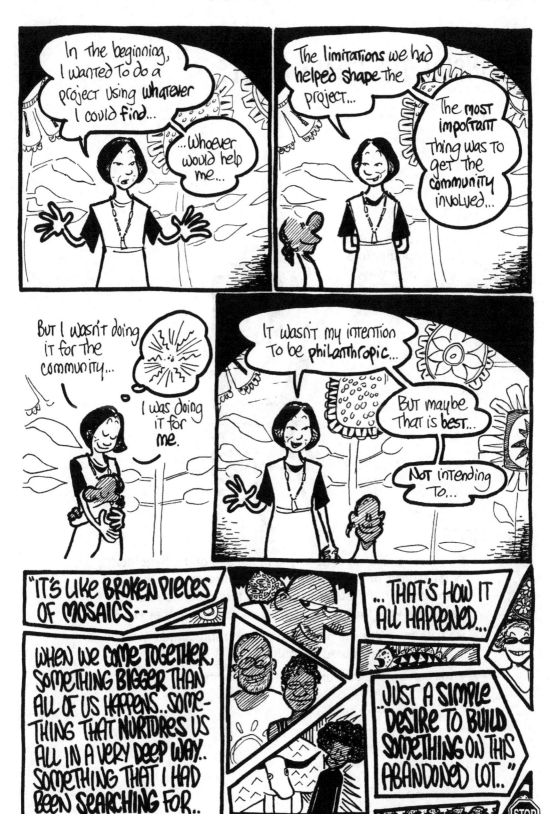

Art by Keith Knight, copyright 2005

INSIDE THE CRAFT CIRCLE

TIP

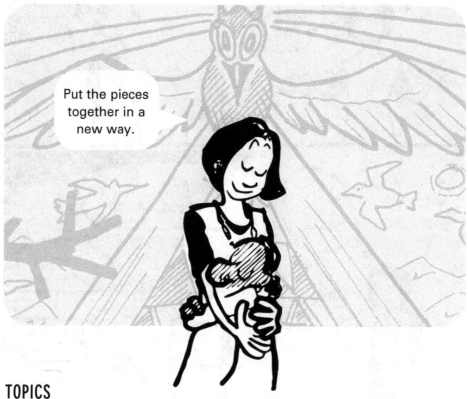

TOPICS

- Discuss the idea that "beauty is in the eye of the beholder." What aspects of the community environment do some members of the group find beautiful that others do not? Can those who find something ugly see it in another way?

- How do the values of a community get represented in what is and is not considered beautiful?

- What can an outsider bring to a community?

TECHNIQUE: THE "IT PULLS IT ALL APART" APPROACH*

Derived from exercises of the Village of Arts & Humanities Theater Program,
Philadelphia, PA

DURATION
  3 to 6 months

OBJECTIVES
  • Art: Create a musical theater piece as a unified group expression.
  • Learning: Compare, contrast and interweave disparate ideas and
    perspectives.
  • Social Change: Create a common experience as a touchstone to give
    audiences the chance to celebrate their interconnections.

MATERIALS
  • Video camera and monitor (or audio recorder only)
  • Computer with word processing program
  • Rehearsal space
  • Performance space with some lighting capability
  • Sets, props, sound, etc.

STEPS
  1. Form a group of teens large enough for the show you would like
     to produce. The company will need to include an adult director and
     playwright.

  2. Choose common questions to use as a topic for the performance,
     such as "What keeps people apart even when they live in the same
     community?"

  3. Based on these questions, work as a group to conduct and record
     interviews with different types of people in the community (elders,
     children, mothers, workers, professionals, students, etc.).

  4. Director and playwright to review the recordings and develop an initial
     story outline.

CONTINUED

*Named for the first play the Village created using this approach, directed by German Wilson

5. Based on the outline, begin rehearsals where the group improvises, with members trying on different characters. Then discuss each scene as a group: Was it believable? Was it engaging? What could be done differently? Could it – should it – be funnier? More dramatic?

6. After each workshop, have the playwright review rehearsal videotape and develop a script.

7. Continue reworking each scene until the script feels complete. Assign names to the characters and cast actors in each role.

8. Begin working on choreography, music, and other dramatic elements.

9. Create simple props, costumes, backdrops, and lighting as needed.

10. Present the performance to the community.

VARIATIONS
- Use this same process to create and exhibit community murals, quilts, and other projects.
- Start out with a small group and use the community interview process to help recruit performers.

NOTES
- Even the most collaborative theater projects, usually require at least one professional leader as director. The director's job is to tap into the spirit and ideas of the teen participants, to incorporate their excitement, honesty and input. Keep in mind, the participants must experience ownership of the project, otherwise it won't work.

Seattle, Washington is our next stop.

Known as the Emerald City, this town excels in livability.

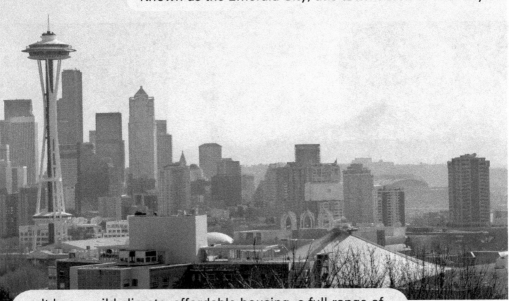

It has a mild climate, affordable housing, a full range of arts, culture and sporting events, an abundance of shops and restaurants, and easy access to outdoor recreational activities throughout the year. In short, a good place for the good life.

In such a livable town, you would think opportunities for cultural expression would be in abundance, particularly among Filipino Americans, the largest Asian American Pacific Islander group in the area. But this is not always so in the Emerald City.

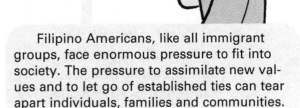

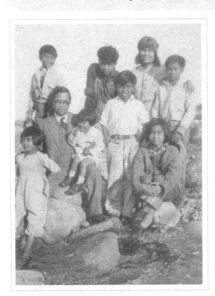

Filipino Americans, like all immigrant groups, face enormous pressure to fit into society. The pressure to assimilate new values and to let go of established ties can tear apart individuals, families and communities.

Building connections across generations and perspectives is one way to help to keep this from happening.

One group of artists has come up with an inspired strategy
– bring people together through Love.

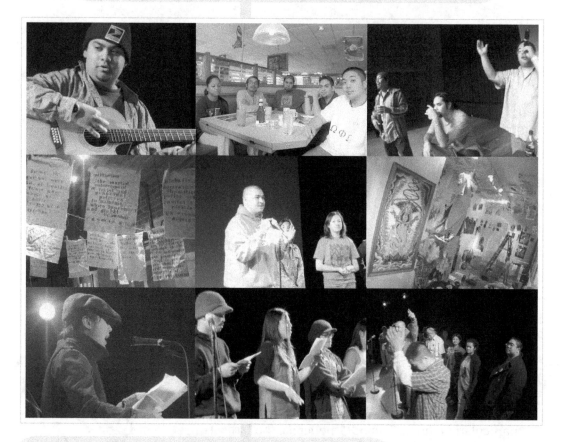

Starting as a Filipino-based organization, the group has expanded to welcome members from all cultures and audiences from all ages, backgrounds and perspectives.

Meeting at the crossroads of spoken word, dance, music and visual art, **Isangmahal Arts Kollective** creates events that celebrate and activate their community. Get to know these social visionaries in the story we call **"One Love."**

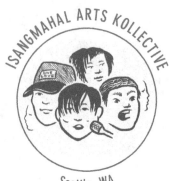

Seattle, WA

isangmahal arts kollective

IS MADE UP OF SEATTLE POETS, RAPPERS, DANCERS, SINGERS, DEEJAYS, MUSICIANS, AND ACTORS WHO SHARE A BELIEF IN **LOVE** AS THE ESSENTIAL INGREDIENT IN **SOCIAL CHANGE.**

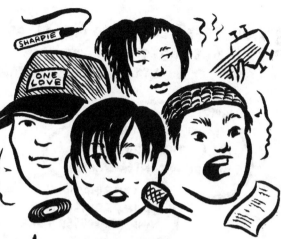

⌐HEIR PURPOSE:
TO HEAR AND BE HEARD...
TO SEE AND BE SEEN.

⌐HE ORIGIN OF ISANG MAHAL* CAME OUT OF A ONE-SHOT CULTURAL EVENT CALLED **ALL-ONE TRIBE** IN 1996.

THE IDEA WAS TO PRODUCE A SERIES OF THEMED SHOWS THAT HONORED DIFFERENT COMMUNITY ACTIVISTS & ORGANIZATIONS, AND TO BUILD **CONNECTIONS** BETWEEN **ORGANIZATIONS.**

OUR EVENTS **ARE** OUR ART...

WHO IS IN THE ROOM AND WHAT OUR PROGRAM MEANS TO THEM IS AS IMPORTANT TO US AS WHAT'S GOING ON ONSTAGE.

jojo gaon

OUR AUDIENCES CROSS **AGES, COLORS, CLASSES, & POLITICS.** PEOPLE JOIN WITH US AS SOON AS THEY DECIDE THEY WANT TO.

IT'S A SAFE, CREATIVE SPACE THAT AUDIENCES CAN'T FIND ANYPLACE ELSE.

* "ISANG MAHAL" = "ONE LOVE"

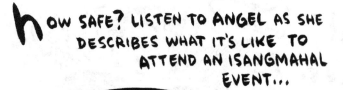

hOW SAFE? LISTEN TO ANGEL AS SHE DESCRIBES WHAT IT'S LIKE TO ATTEND AN ISANGMAHAL EVENT...

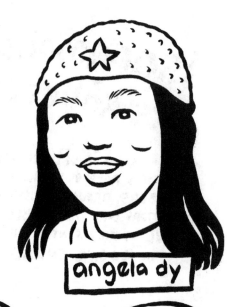

angela dy

MAN, YOU'VE GOT **ALL** THESE DIFFERENT DISCIPLINES INTERACTING...

A COMBINATION OF IMPROVISATION AND REHEARSED WORKS.

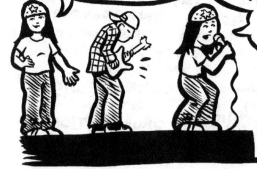

MUSICIANS APPEAR BEHIND YOU AND THEY ARE TOTALLY THERE FOR YOU...

...RESPONDING TO WHAT THEY RECEIVE FROM YOUR POETRY...

AND YOU DO THE SAME...

THERE'S NO REAL SEPARATION BETWEEN ARTISTS & AUDIENCE...

AT THAT MOMENT, WE ARE ALL **ISANG MAHAL**.

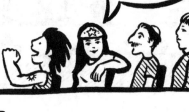

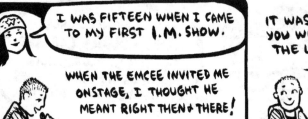

I WAS FIFTEEN WHEN I CAME TO MY FIRST I.M. SHOW.

WHEN THE EMCEE INVITED ME ONSTAGE, I THOUGHT HE MEANT RIGHT THEN & THERE!

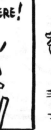

IT WAS SO UNUSUAL TO BE INVITED... IT MAKES YOU WANT TO BE A PART OF THE GROUP FOR THE LONG HAUL.

OF COURSE, IT WASN'T UNTIL WEEKS LATER THAT I LEARNED I HAD UNKNOWINGLY ADDED MYSELF TO A **REHEARSED** PERFORMANCE.

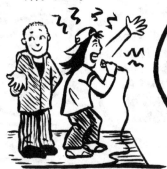

Art by Ellen Forney, copyright 2005

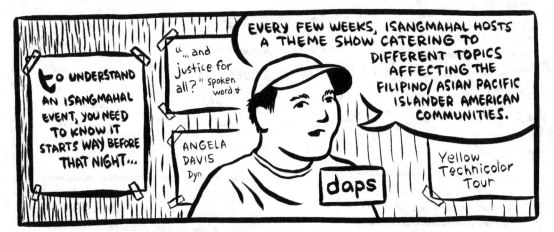

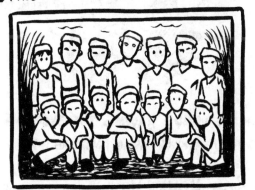

THE GOAL OF THE BILL WAS TO PROVIDE FULL EQUITY TO FILIPINO VETERANS.

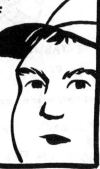

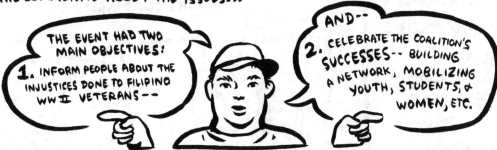

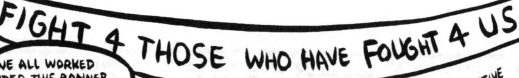

FIGHT 4 THOSE WHO HAVE FOUGHT 4 US

WE ALL WORKED UNDER THIS BANNER OF UNDERSTANDING,

As HOST FOR THIS EVENT, ISANGMAHAL ARTS KOLLECTIVE BECAME RESPONSIBLE FOR A QUALITY SHOW. THIS INVOLVES MANY DIFFERENT ELEMENTS, INCLUDING PROGRAMMING, PUBLICITY, FINDING ARTISTS TO PERFORM, & COMMUNICATING WITH THEATER STAFF.

FIRST: OBJECTIVES FOR THE SHOW ARE LAID OUT.

SECOND: WE DECIDE A SET OF BASIC, PRACTICAL QUESTIONS.

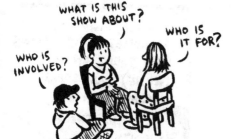

WHAT IS THIS SHOW ABOUT?

WHO IS IT FOR?

WHO IS INVOLVED?

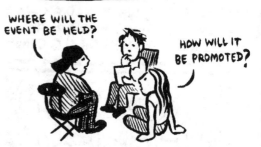

WHERE WILL THE EVENT BE HELD?

HOW WILL IT BE PROMOTED?

ESTABLISHING A RELATIONSHIP WITH THE VENUE HAVING THE EVENT IS EXTREMELY IMPORTANT-- IN THIS CASE, THE NORTHWEST ASIAN AMERICAN THEATER.

To HAVE A GREAT SHOW, WE TRY TO STIMULATE AS MANY OF THE AUDIENCE'S SENSES AS POSSIBLE: **SIGHTS, SOUNDS, TEXTURES, TASTES,** AND SOMETIMES, **SMELLS!**

For THIS EVENT, **HOVEN VIDA,** A GRAFFITI ARTIST & ISANGMAHAL MEMBER, PROVIDED A GREAT BACKDROP OF A FILIPINO WW II VET, WITH SMALL CARICATURES HOLDING BLANK PICKET SIGNS THAT ANYONE COULD WRITE SLOGANS IN.

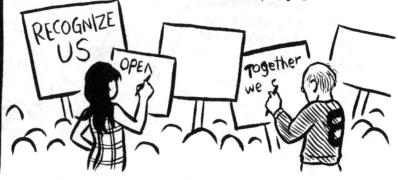

RECOGNIZE US

OPEN

Together we

Art by Ellen Forney, copyright 2005

For every theme show, a few members of isangmahal agree to act as the point people for that event. They determine when the doors will open, what time the show will begin, set up the order of the performers, and provide responsibilities to volunteers and isangmahal members.

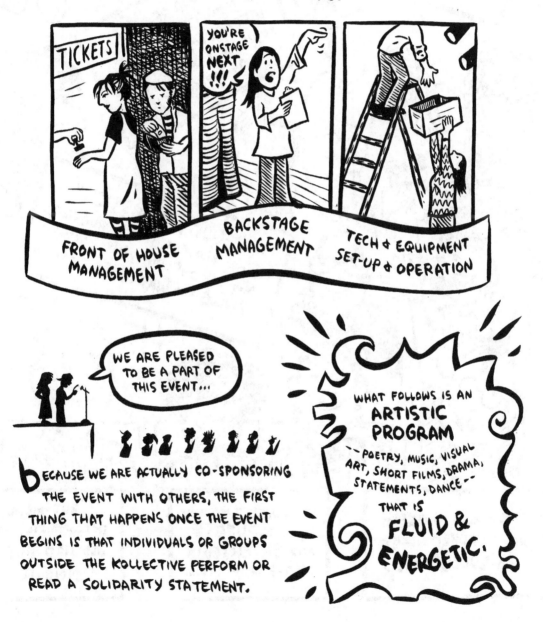

FRONT OF HOUSE MANAGEMENT

BACKSTAGE MANAGEMENT

TECH & EQUIPMENT SET-UP & OPERATION

Because we are actually co-sponsoring the event with others, the first thing that happens once the event begins is that individuals or groups outside the kollective perform or read a solidarity statement.

What follows is an ARTISTIC PROGRAM -- poetry, music, visual art, short films, drama, statements, dance -- that is FLUID & ENERGETIC.

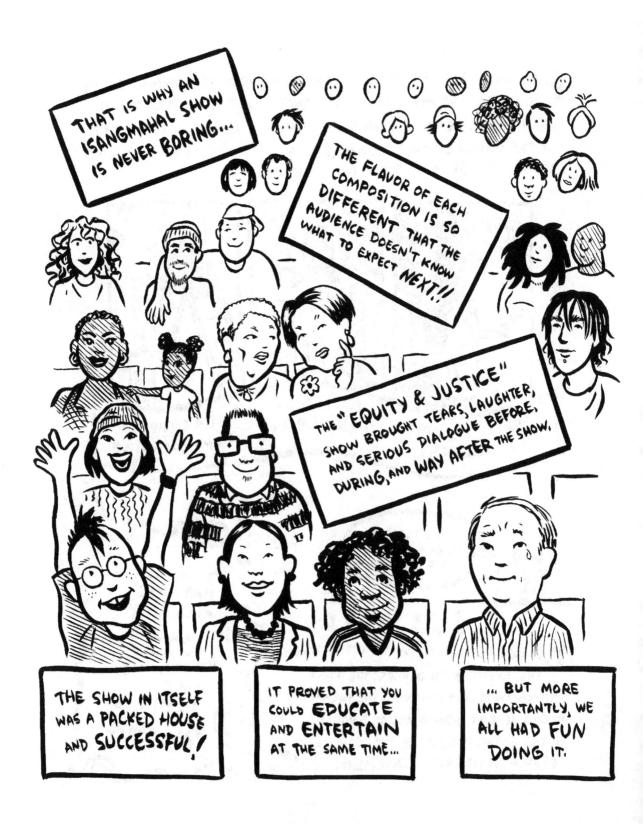

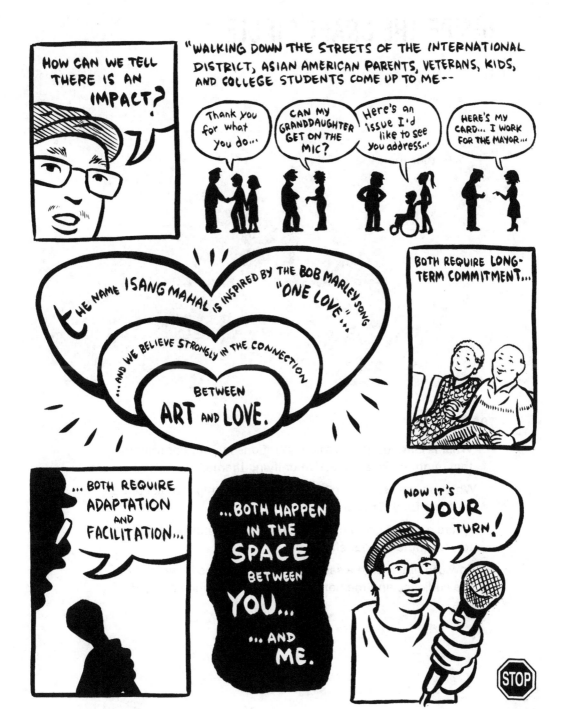

Art by Ellen Forney, copyright 2005

INSIDE THE CRAFT CIRCLE

TIP

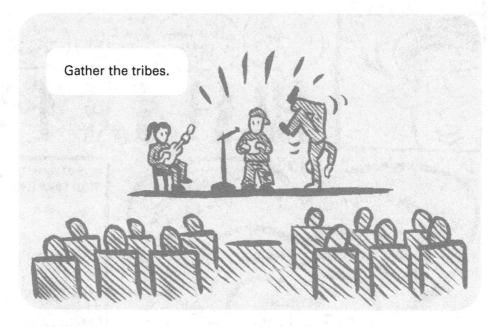

Gather the tribes.

TOPICS

- What issues cut across the generations in your community that might make an effective unifying theme?
- What groups associated with those issues might make good partners for your project?
- Where can you go to find artists and performers with ideas to contribute to your show?
- How can you create a safe performance space in which both the audience and the performers are active and engaged?

TECHNIQUE: THEME SHOWS

Derived from exercises of Isangmahal Arts Kollective, Seattle, WA

DURATION

3-hour event, minimum 12 weeks advance planning

OBJECTIVE

- Art: Provide a showcase for the community's gifts, skills, and talents.
- Learning: Stimulate community-wide reflection.
- Social change: Bring people together to take action.

MATERIALS

- Rehearsal and meeting space
- Necessary supplies for marketing and promotion
- Performance space
- Sets, props, sound and lighting technology

STEPS

Weeks 1-2: Contact

- Form a group of five or six people responsible for organizing the event (see NOTES for details).

- In group discussion, agree upon a theme for the show and create a production timeline.

- Contact potential partners in the community.

Week 3-6: Research

- Recruit poets, dancers, musicians, visual artists, etc.

- Interview members of the community – include people from different generations – who are connected to the theme.   Pass along the results to the artists.

Week 5-11: Action

- Provide artist support, such as rehearsal space and a stipend for supplies if possible.

- Ask artists to create vignettes or monologues based on the interview material.

- Organize group rehearsals where artists create, share and strengthen connections between the pieces.

CONTINUED

Week 9-12: Feedback

- Facilitate social change action the audience can take the night of the event, such as writing letters, making phone calls, signing petitions, committing to talk with elected officials, planning future events, etc.

- Create buzz by enlisting artists, community partners, and the media.

Week 12: Teaching

- Fine-tune your "talking points" about the issues.

- Showtime!

The event consists of 2 main elements:

- Feature Set: A 90-minute series of short pieces developed by the artists as described above

- Open Mic: A 90-minute session for new works in progress (performers sign up on the night of the show)

FOLLOW-UP/VARIATIONS

- Use the Open Mic to recruit artists for the next Theme Show.
- In addition to theme shows, Isangmahal also organizes open shows, which present a mixture of poetry, dance, music, and art on topics of the artist's choice. Less time is needed to produce such a show – about four weeks – but the procedure is the same.

NOTES

- Event Organizing Group: Within this group of 5-6 people, you will need individuals to play various roles.
- Two Point People: One will focus on production issues such as outreach, facilities, schedules, house management, and stage management. The other will focus on the technical requirements for the show (lights, sound, costumes, venue). Both work to coordinate publicity.
- The remaining members will concentrate on the program, recruiting and supporting artists.

FEEDBACK

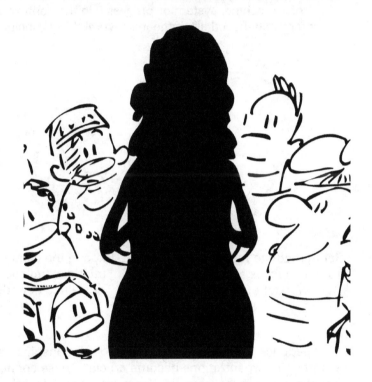

Spark reflection, dialogue and organizing
to spread the impact of the new art work.

Whew!

From "Action" has come a new work of art, perhaps a new concept for change within the community. Having successfully climbed a steep incline it's time to level off, and turn that accomplishment into something more.

It's time to get the word out, to circulate the new work of art within the community. Now we're in **Feedback** territory.

In the dictionary, Feedback is defined as "The return to the input of a machine, system or process." In the context of community-based art, it means several things, including:

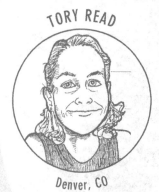

TORY READ

Denver, CO

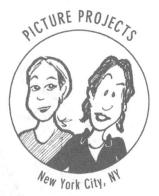

PICTURE PROJECTS

New York City, NY

Get immediate responses from audiences about the work(s) of art.

Expand the dialogue among multiple audiences over a sustained period of time.

Feedback is the place where strong relationships with community organizations become crucial. These connections make possible the transition from a successful work of art to a successful campaign for community change.

As leader, it will be important for you to begin thinking about Feedback ahead of time. Feedback is probably the most difficult CRAFT concept to understand, so you need to really be on top of things – become an audience member and advocate for the new work even before the group fully understands what it is going to create.

For some, the work of Feedback will never be as glamorous or exciting as Action, but it is perhaps the single most important territory of CRAFT – the point at which art connects with mobilizing community-wide resources and energy.

Almost every American city has a neighborhood dubbed something like "the murder capitol." These nicknames are sometimes based on fact, but more often than not they are built on stereotypes and half-truths. Regardless of reality, once they are picked up by the mass media, these images can become true by reinforcing hopelessness, despair and apathy.

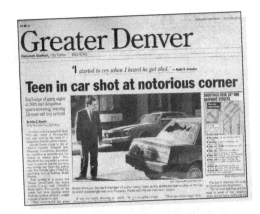

Greater Denver

'I started to cry when I heard he got shot.'

Teen in car shot at notorious corner

Denver, Colorado
is our next destination.

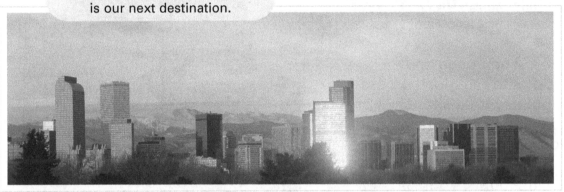

About 500,000 people, 154 square miles in area, 5,280 feet elevation. Also known as the "Mile-High City." Major industries are communications, utilities and transportation.

Denver has long prided itself on being a city of quaint neighborhoods filled with solid, safe brick houses:

Barnum, Clement's Addition, Elyria Swansea, Hampden Heights, Harvey Park, Whittier and Wellshire, to name a few.

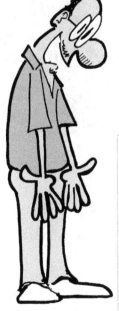

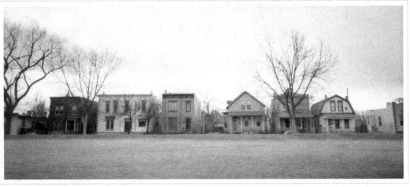

A few years ago, if you lived in or around Denver, the name "Curtis Park" went along with very different images, like police sirens, children's screams and screeching tires.

How about it: When the anchorman reports only negative events in your neighborhood, do you ever find yourself talking back to the television?

When page one neglects to mention successes, but never fails to focus on the failures, do you ever find yourself wishing you could **"Talk Back"** to the public yourself?

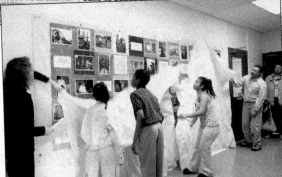

"*Our children are dying. What I would like people to do is ask themselves the question, 'Can I do anything?' Then do it. Joey could have been your kid.*"
— **Stephanie Wilson**, City Park Cedars treatment program for youths

Boy shot in Curtis Park dies

Police declare war on gangs after fourth recent slaying near deadly intersection

By John C. Ensslin
Rocky Mountain News Staff Writer

Police launched a major crackdown against gangs near a deadly Denver street corner Friday as a 15-year-old boy became the area's fourth slaying victim in four months.

Joseph Green was shot in the back of the head Thursday after a midday snow-football game gave way to a gang confrontation at 26th and Arapahoe streets. He died Friday.

Police brass vowed a swift, aggressive campaign against gang members and drug dealers in the neighborhood.

The crackdown, begun Friday night, includes:

■ Assigning the 30-officer Denver gang bureau and an undisclosed number of extra officers from District 6 to the Curtis Park neighborhood full time.

■ Launc neighborho was to have

INSIDE
■ Shooting wipes out a dream of adoption /32A

Joseph Green, 15, left, died Friday after being shot Thursday in the head at 26th and Arapahoe streets, in the Curtis Park neighborhood. Right, Stephanie Wilson, director of the City Park Cedars treatment program for youths, talks about Green, who had been a client.

Calls to police paint
statement. "Unfortunately, he was in the

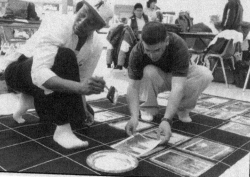

Residents' neighborhood photos speak eloquently of realities, joys
By Jeff Bradley
groups, merchants and the Colorado

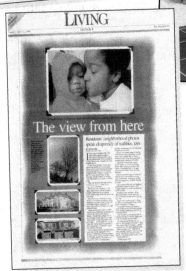

LIVING

The view from here

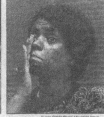

TORY READ

Denver, CO

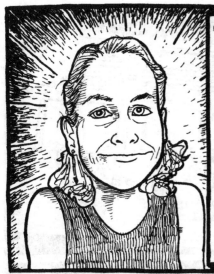

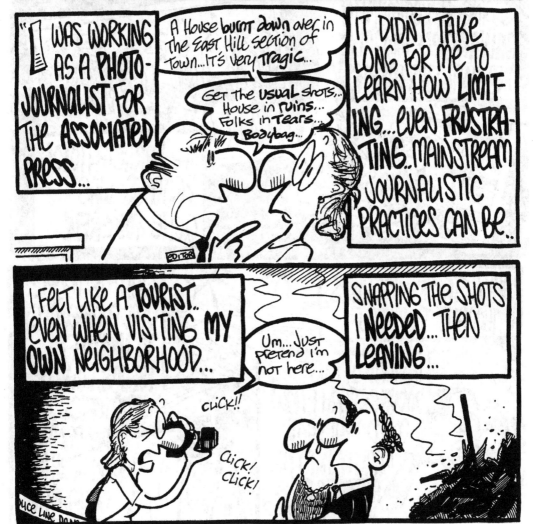

Art by Keith Knight, copyright 2005

I TOOK SOME TIME OFF TO TRAVEL TO **INDONESIA** WHERE I DOCUMENTED AN EXPERIMENTAL COMMUNITY-BASED REFORESTATION PROJECT...

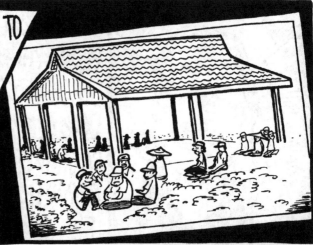

SEEING A COMMUNITY GALVANIZED TOWARDS ONE GOAL WAS **INSPIRING**

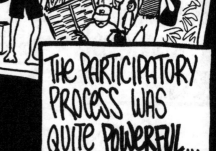

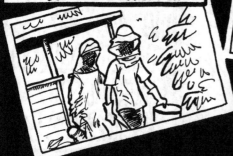

THE PARTICIPATORY PROCESS WAS QUITE **POWERFUL**...

WHILE TAKING PICTURES, I THOUGHT TO MYSELF:

INSTEAD OF JUST DOCUMENTING IT, HOW COULD I PUT PHOTO-GRAPHY INTO AN ACTIVIST ROLE IN THE PROCESS?

WHAT IF PEOPLE USED PHOTOGRAPHY TO **IDENTIFY** ISSUES, DEVELOP STRATEGIES, & SOLVE PROBLEMS WITHIN THEIR OWN COMMUNITIES?

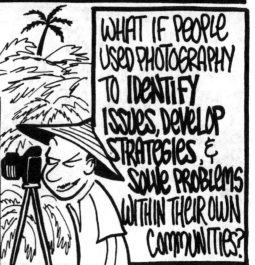

Art by Keith Knight, copyright 2005

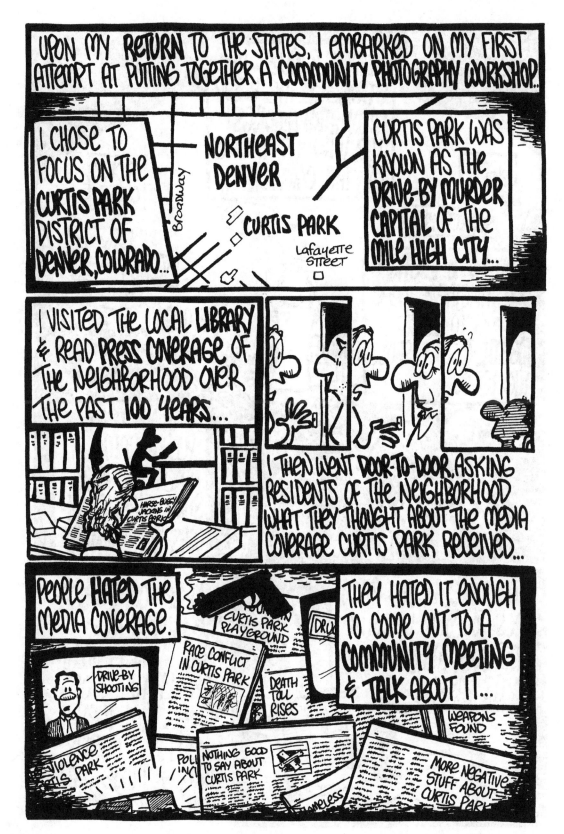

Art by Keith Knight, copyright 2005

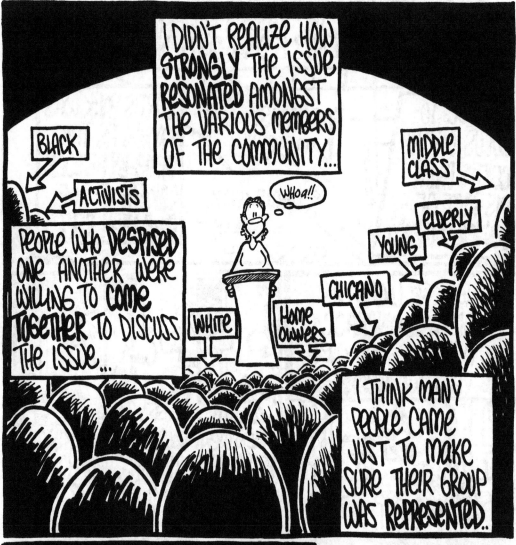

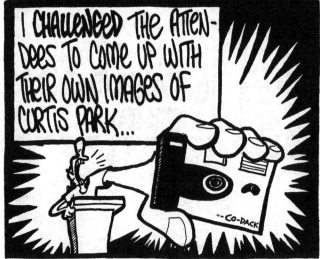

ONE OF THE PHOTOS THAT STOOD OUT FROM THAT PROJECT WAS OF **GRAFFITI**, TAKEN BY ONE OF THE **TEENS** FROM THE NEIGHBORHOOD...

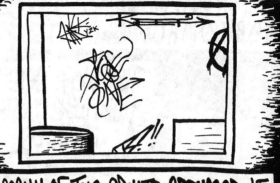

MANY OF THE ADULTS ASSUMED IT WAS SOMETHING THE TEENAGER **LOVED** ABOUT CURTIS PARK...

BUT IN FACT, IT WAS SOMETHING HE WANTED TO **CHANGE**...

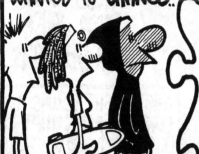

SUDDENLY, THINGS WEREN'T SO **SIMPLE** FOR THE ADULTS...

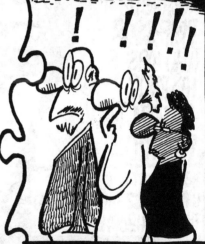

! ! ! ! !

THEY NOW HAD TO **RETHINK** THEIR ASSUMPTIONS ABOUT THE YOUNG FOLKS IN THE NEIGHBORHOOD...

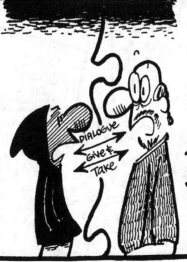

DIALOGUE
GIVE & TAKE

HERE WAS A **CLEAR** EXAMPLE OF HOW PHOTOGRAPHY COULD GET **DIFFERENT** KINDS OF PEOPLE **TALKING** WHO THINK THEY KNOW **EVERYTHING** ABOUT EACH OTHER, BUT IN REALITY, KNOW **VERY LITTLE**....

Art by Keith Knight, copyright 2005

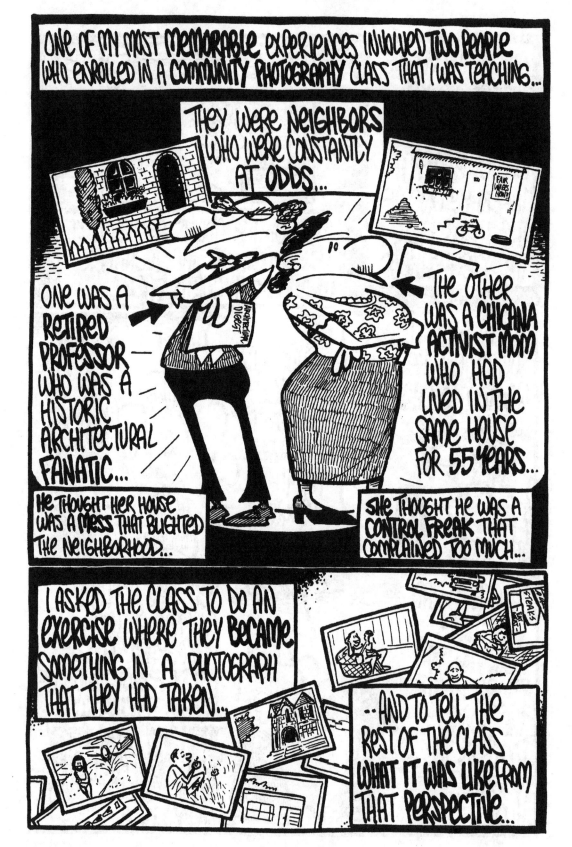

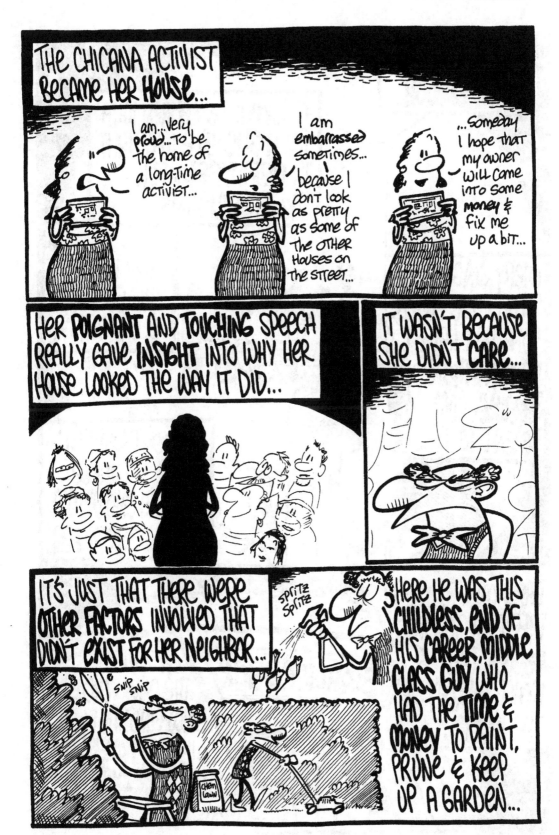

Art by Keith Knight, copyright 2005

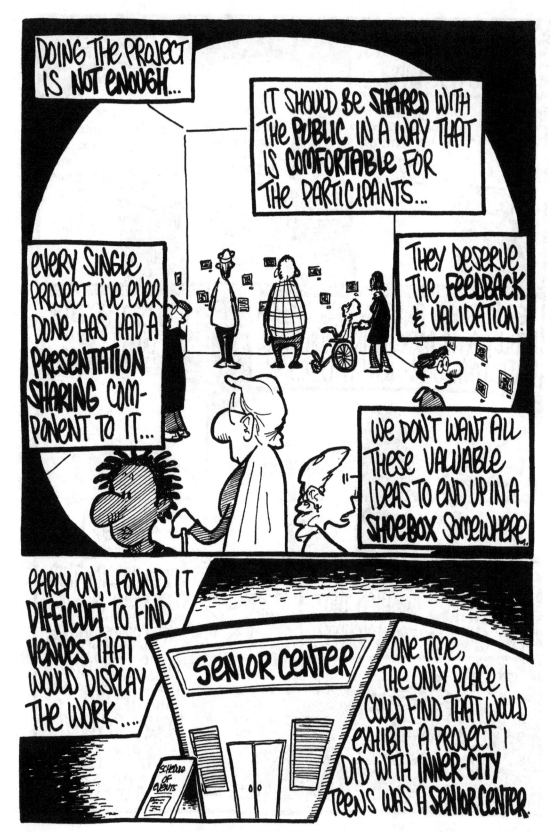

Art by Keith Knight, copyright 2005

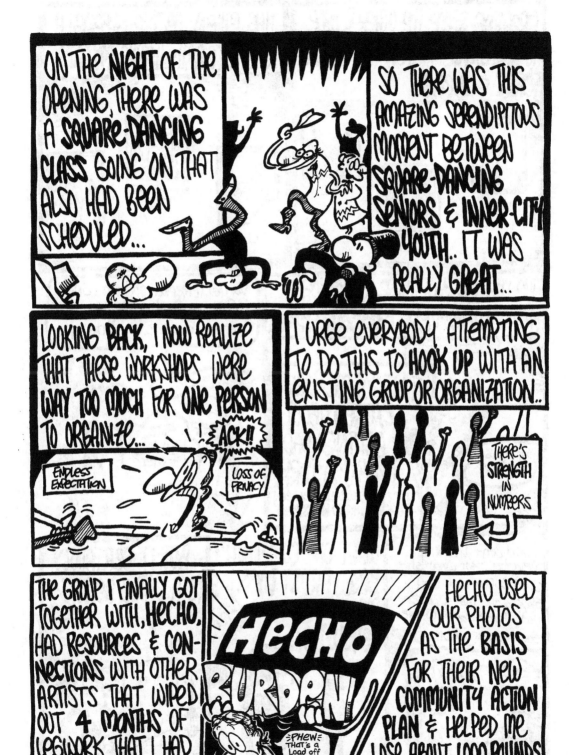

Art by Keith Knight, copyright 2005

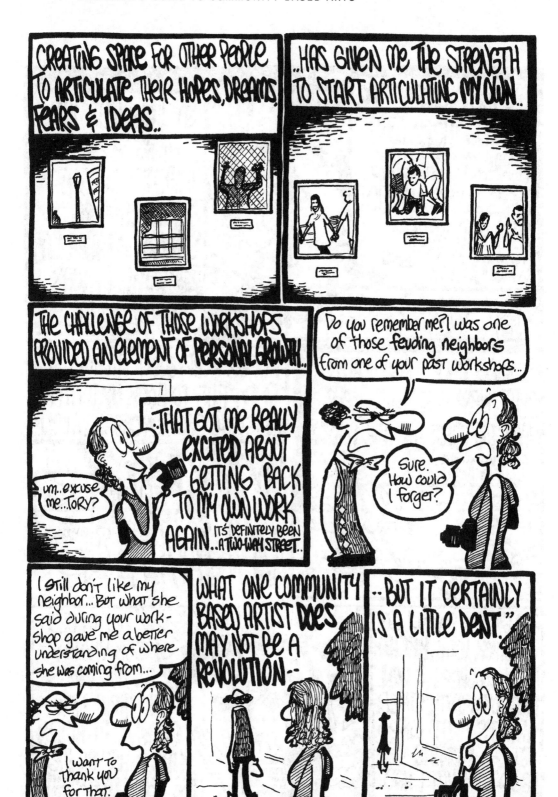

Art by Keith Knight, copyright 2005

INSIDE THE CRAFT CIRCLE

TIP

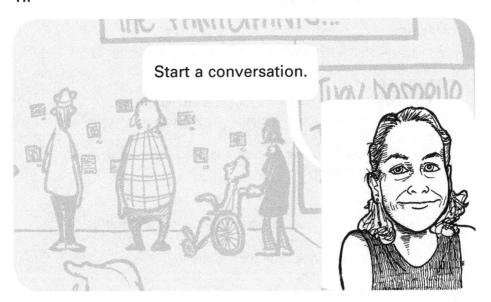

Start a conversation.

TOPICS

- Who is the most important audience for your new artistic product(s)?
- What communications media do these audiences use most? Be sure to include both mass media (radio, television, etc.) and more localized media (meetings, parades, street posts, the water cooler).
- What community groups might partner with you to build your audience?
- How can art provide an alternative information source to mainstream media?

TECHNIQUE: TALK BACK! EVENT

Derived from exercises of Tory Read, Denver, CO

DURATION
    3 to 4 hour event, minimum 8 weeks advance planning

OBJECTIVES
    • Art: Develop ability to think about and discuss art.
    • Learning: Analyze how the media covers your community or group.
    • Social Change: Influence the way the media represents you and your community.

MATERIALS
    • A public space that has wall space and lots of foot traffic
    • Food, live music by community musicians
    • Nametags, guest sign-in/comment book
    • Public Address system

STEPS

1. Create a body of artwork – such as photographs, dances, paintings, audio pieces – that relate to the group's chosen issues, or perceptions of the community in the media.

2. Include lots of group discussions along the way, so that everyone gets comfortable with talking about their work in front of others and feels their contributions are appreciated.

3. Allowing at least two months' lead-time, establish a convenient day, time, and place for a "Talk Back" gathering.

4. Send out invitations to community members, reporters, and public officials.

5. Send out press releases to radio, TV, and newspapers.

6. Personally call and invite reporters and public officials the day before the event.

7. Ask group members to take on roles, including greeters, artwork tour guides, interviewers set-up and clean-up crew.

AGENDA
- Schedule free time for guests to experience the art on their own, using participants as hosts and interpreters. Offer music, food. (1 to 2 hours. Can precede or follow the program.)
- Welcome and explain the process. (10 minutes)
- Facilitate a panel discussion in which three or four representatives of the neighborhood and your group speak about the art and the issues. (30 minutes)
- Invite media and audience members to ask questions, comment about the artwork, express concerns, and give other feedback. (30 minutes)
- Challenge people to take action. Ask those in positions of influence (journalists, editors, elected officials) in the audience, as well as everyone else, what they will do differently as a result of the discussion. (15 minutes)
- Give a closing thank you statement. Encourage participants to sign the guest book and include their addresses so you can invite them to future events. (15 minutes)

VARIATION
- Partner with a community action group looking for feedback on the same issue.

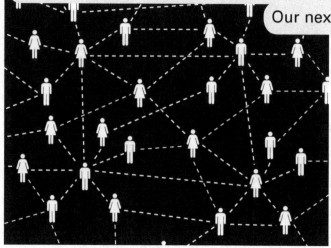

Up until now, we have concentrated on communities defined by place.

Our next story changes that.

The impact of the **Internet** on our thoughts and feelings about community cannot be over-estimated. Once, all human beings had a notion of community (and life itself) as place-based; most still do. But with the advent of online communications, that is changing.

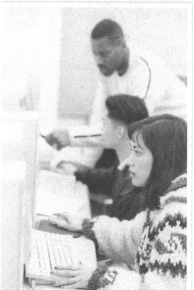

Now, more than ever before, it is possible for people who have never met before in person to have complex, long-term, productive, even intimate relationships – in short, community. The traditional face-to-face activities of the old-time community square: business, government, religion, public speech, even marriages, are being conducted increasingly online.

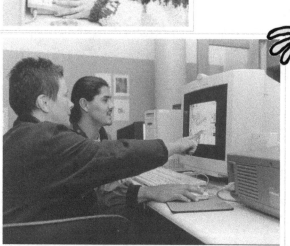

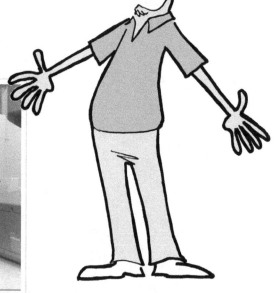

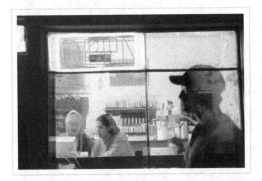

Still, millions of Americans do not spend much or any time in digital communities, and even those who do also participate in their real-world communities and relationships (at least enough to get a loaf of bread). The full impact of these changes remains to be seen, but there can be little doubt that change is under way.

Artists, too, have started experimenting with the community-building potential of the online medium.

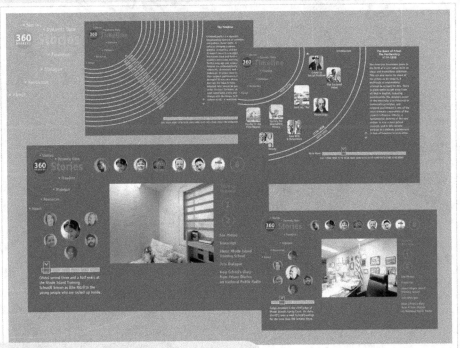

One such group of digital documentary artists, based in New York City and located on the Web at www.360degrees.org, uses the Internet as an interactive, instantaneous distribution system, building connections between unlikely groups of people, and then following it up with face-to-face action.

Meet some artists who have created **"A Town Hall in Cyber Space."**

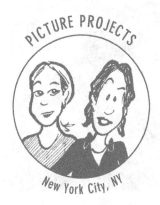

PICTURE PROJECTS

New York City, NY

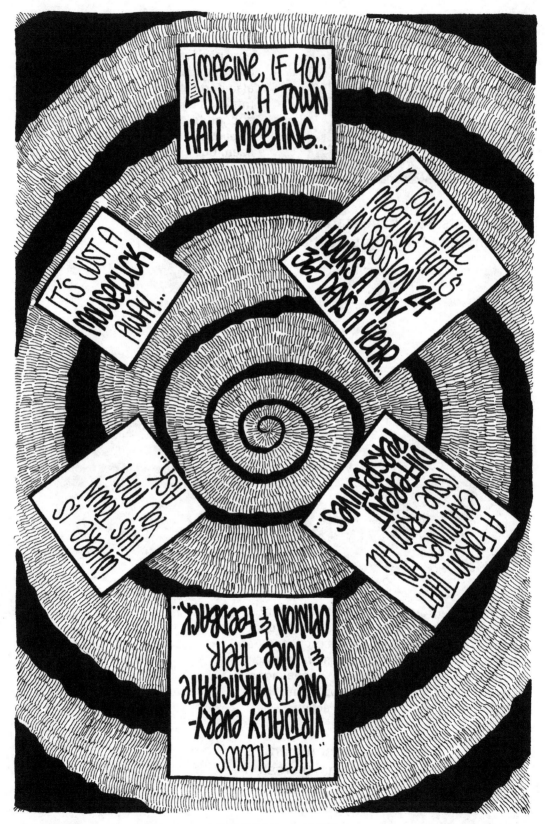

Art by Keith Knight, copyright 2005

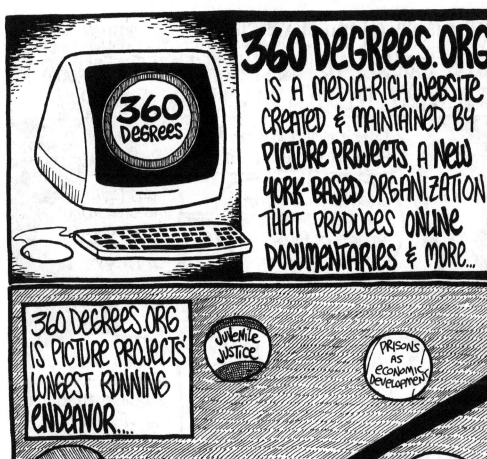

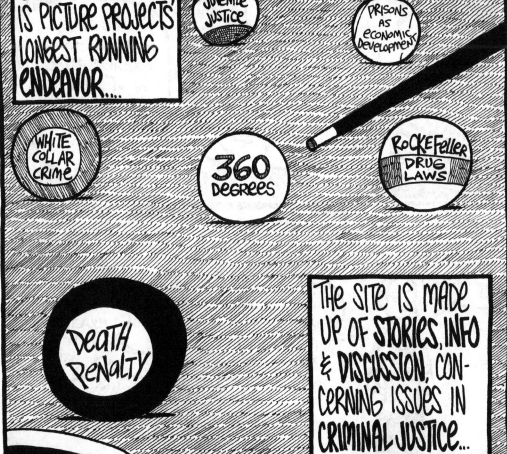

Art by Keith Knight, copyright 2005

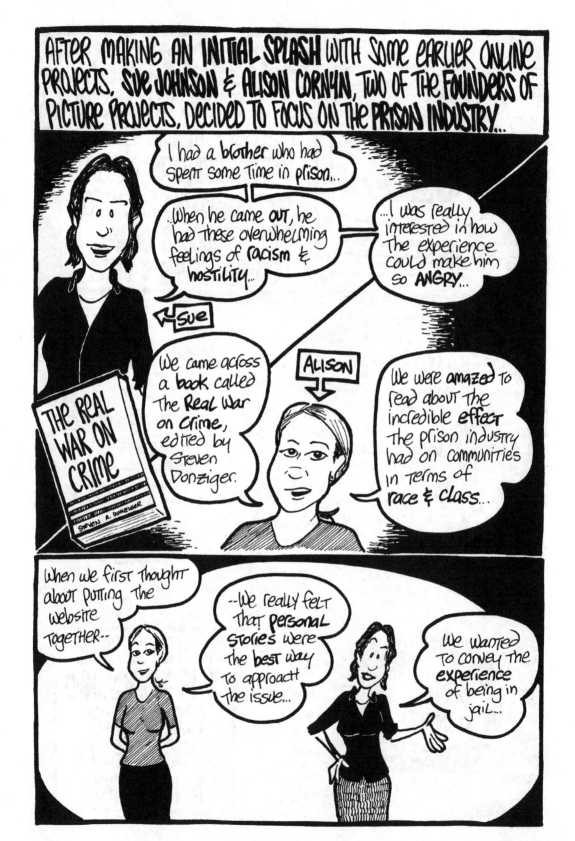

Art by Keith Knight, copyright 2005

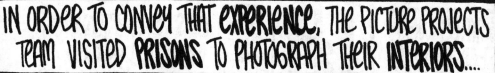

IN ORDER TO CONVEY THAT **EXPERIENCE**, THE PICTURE PROJECTS TEAM VISITED **PRISONS** TO PHOTOGRAPH THEIR **INTERIORS**....

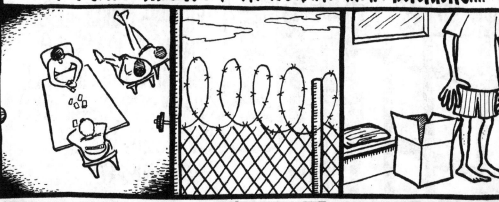

THE **STORIES SECTION** OF 360DEGREES.ORG TAKES **FULL ADVANTAGE** OF THE WEB MEDIUM, GIVING THE VISITOR A **MULTI-VANTAGED VIEW** OF THE **PRISON EXPERIENCE**..

Clicking one's cursor on any photo triggers access to photos, video, audio & text...

JEROME

RETIRED JUDGE

NESTOR

PROSECUTOR

DARRYL

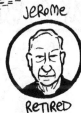

PRISONER

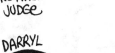
..whenever I get out of here, the first thing I'm gonna do is fight to get the law changed...

WANDA

PRISONER'S WIFE

FORMER DIRECTOR OF CRIMINAL JUSTICE

We wanted to show this **incredible** network of people who participate in or make decisions about the criminal justice system **every day**....

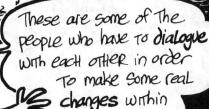

These are some of the people who have to **dialogue** with each other in order to make some real changes within the system.

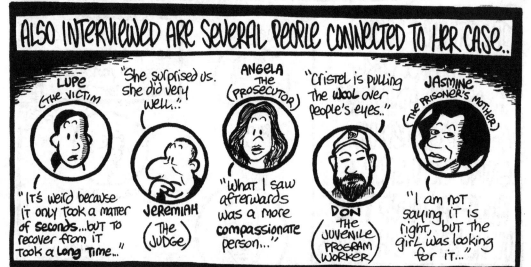

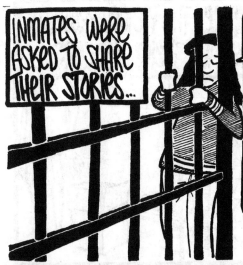

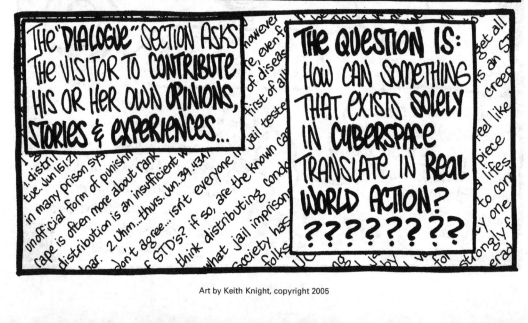

Art by Keith Knight, copyright 2005

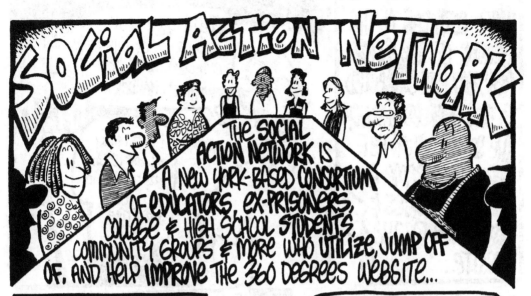

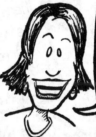

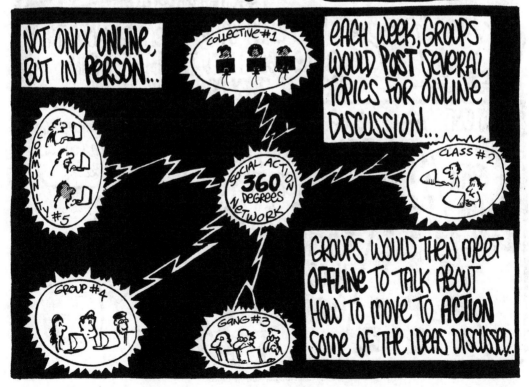

Art by Keith Knight, copyright 2005

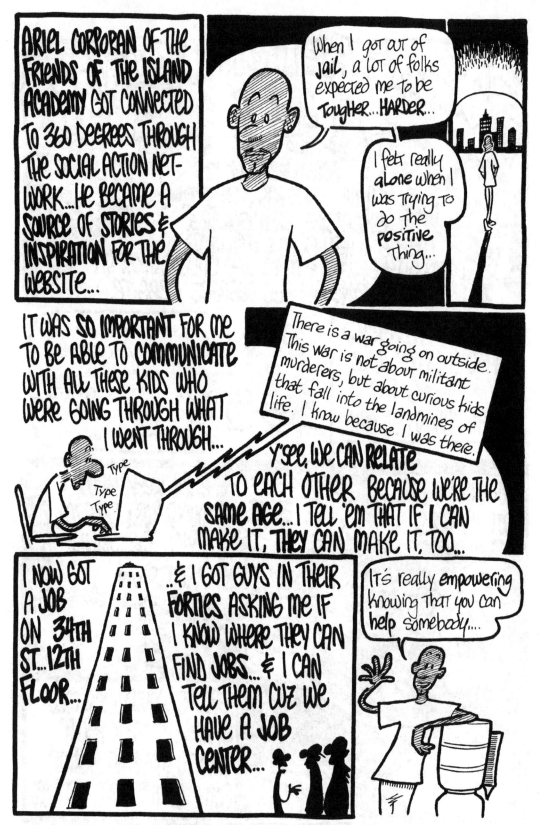

Art by Keith Knight, copyright 2005

CARL JOHNSON TOOK PART IN THE SOCIAL ACTION NETWORK WHILE AT THE FORTUNE SOCIETY... HE IS NOW IN BUSINESS FOR HIMSELF....

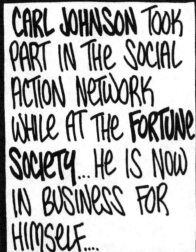

Through 360 degrees, I got interested in social issues...

Participating helped me personally gain confidence in myself...

...Transforming me from someone who had been incarcerated & warehoused... to someone productive & useful...

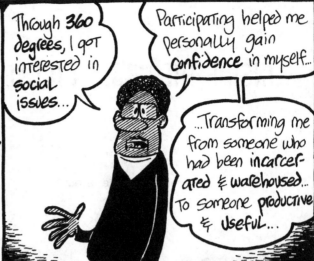

HER STORY... HIS STORY... YOUR STORY. THE CREATORS OF THE 360 DEGREES WEBSITE HOPE THAT EVERY STORY, IDEA & OPINION SHARED ON THE SITE CREATES A RIPPLE EFFECT...

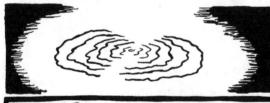

A RIPPLE THAT AFFECTS EVERY PERSON IT COMES INTO CONTACT WITH, GAINING MOMENTUM AS MORE PEOPLE ADD THEIR FEEDBACK & TAKE ACTION...

...CREATING A HUGE WAVE.... POWERFUL ENOUGH TO BREAK DOWN AGING PRISON SYSTEM POLICIES...

CRASH.

..CREATING A SEA OF CHANGE.

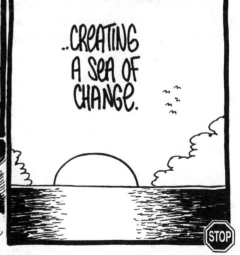

STOP

Art by Keith Knight, copyright 2005

INSIDE THE CRAFT CIRCLE

TIP

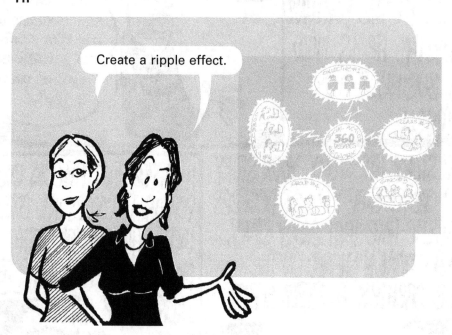

Create a ripple effect.

TOPICS

- Who beyond the primary audience do you want to reach?
- What are your options for reproduction and distribution of your work?
- What changes, if any, in your work will you have to make in order to reach these broader audiences?

TECHNIQUE: THE RIPPLE EFFECT EXERCISE
Derived from exercises of the Picture Projects, New York, NY

DURATION
2 to 3 hours

OBJECTIVES
- Art: Identify a forum that will get your ideas noticed and distributed.
- Learning: Understand formal and informal systems for gathering and disseminating information.
- Social Change: Maximize the impact of your work by reaching people who are not directly connected with the issue, but who can be inspired to respond.

MATERIALS
- Blackboard or large easel pads for group notes
- Paper and pens

STEPS
1. Working with the whole group, create a "Who Cares" ripple-effect map comprised of concentric circles. The center circle represents those most closely connected to the issue of concern to the participants. Moving from the center, each circle represents an audience with less direct involvement.
   This map can include:
   - People like us
   - Family and Friends
   - Acquaintances
   - Community organizations (local non-profit organizations, schools, libraries, newspapers, city government, local businesses)
   - Regional and statewide organizations and agencies
   - National and international organizations and institutions

CONTINUED

2. Divide into small groups of three or four people and distribute writing materials.

3. Have each small group agree upon an issue that concerns them, and make a "Who Cares" map about it. Encourage them to add circles as appropriate to their issue.

4. When the maps are complete, ask each group to discuss the following questions:
   - What communication methods (word of mouth, telephone, e-mail, letter, press conference, website) could be used to spread the word? Who would be helpful in raising awareness of your issue?
   - What action do you want your project to produce? How can an audience be moved to take action?
   - Bring the whole group together after the discussion. Have each small group share their maps and ideas.
   - Commit to taking one action yourself (write a letter to the editor, draft a press release, call a relative or friend and have a conversation about your topic).

FOLLOW-UP / VARIATIONS
- As a reminder to the group, post written materials in a highly visible location.
- Use this exercise when getting started on a project to identify the broadest possible audience.
- After completing a collaborative art piece, use this exercise to inspire a promotional campaign.
- Follow up with updates after you have contacted people about your project or issue.

TEACHING

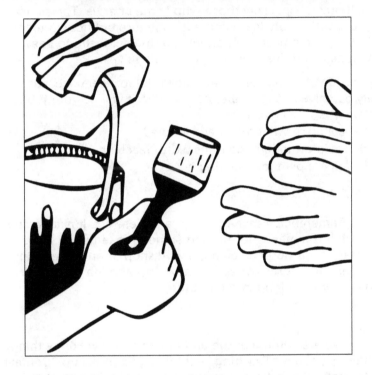

Pass on skills to sustain the impact.

Well, having cultivated, inquired, created and circulated, we are coming to the end of this artistic journey together. We have reached the point where everyone – leader and participant alike – holds the door open for the next person. This is **Teaching** territory.

Teaching – the guiding of someone else's development – goes on all the time. Our world is full of individuals and institutions that want to teach us something.

And listen to this: Teaching, like making art, is something all of us need to do. We all need to be involved in passing on vital information to each other, especially those who come after us. The saying that goes "If you want to truly learn something, figure out how to teach it" has an underlying biological component. Our innate desire to pass on vital information helps motivate us to develop ourselves.

Teaching can be particularly powerful for teens, because youth are so rarely perceived as teachers. As a leader, it will be your job to help participants:

- Reflect upon what they have learned
- Select information and skills worth teaching
- Develop a plan for teaching it

Remember: Teaching is not a selfless act. It is insurance, survival. It is a means for turning something temporary into something long-lasting. Through teaching, a workshop or art project can evolve into a permanent program or even a new organization that continues to have a positive impact long into the future.

We are coming to the end of this journey. Funny thing, though, about "Teaching" – it leads you back into "Contact" territory. You reflect upon what it was like for you at the beginning of the process, and you realize that CRAFT is a kind of circle that positions you to begin another journey.

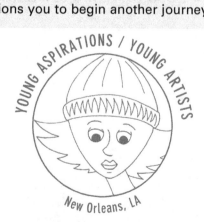

Our journey ends near the Gulf Coast of the United States, in

New Orleans, Louisiana...

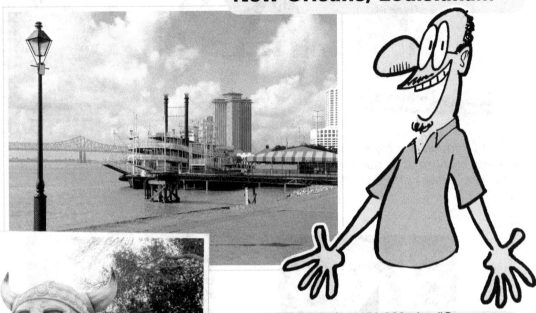

...population 450,000, the "Crescent City," a study in contrasts of epic proportion:

Known throughout the world as a cultural crossroads, birthplace of jazz, the Creole cottage, Cajun zydeco and a $4.5 billion per year tourism industry.

Known throughout the region as an educational dead-end. Less than one-third of the adult population has graduated from high school.

In a city where a world-class tourism industry is built upon a rare sense of local artistry, you would think arts education would be a priority. Still, there is only one music teacher to every three public schools. Fewer still in dance, theater and visual arts.

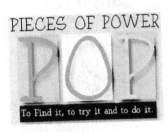

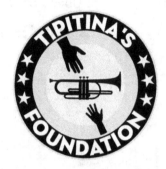

Fortunately for New Orleanians, over the past four decades, dozens of grass-roots arts organizations have sprung up to fill some of this void. They have unique names like "Pieces of Power," "Bamboula 2000" and "Tipitina's Internship Program."

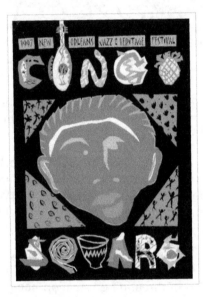

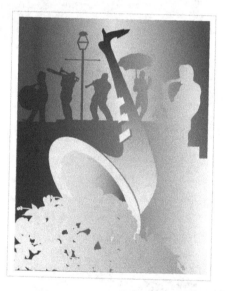

These organizations draw upon the city's rich cultural traditions while incorporating a strong entrepreneurial spirit. Teens are recognized in these programs as innovators and leaders in the creation of new artistic ideas and styles.

"Join Derroles, Johara, Turron, Madania, Andy and program director Rondell Crier, all members of Young Aspirations/ Young Artists visual design guild (YA/YA for short), for one last Tale we call **"Jessie's Story."**

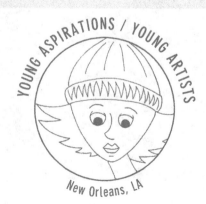

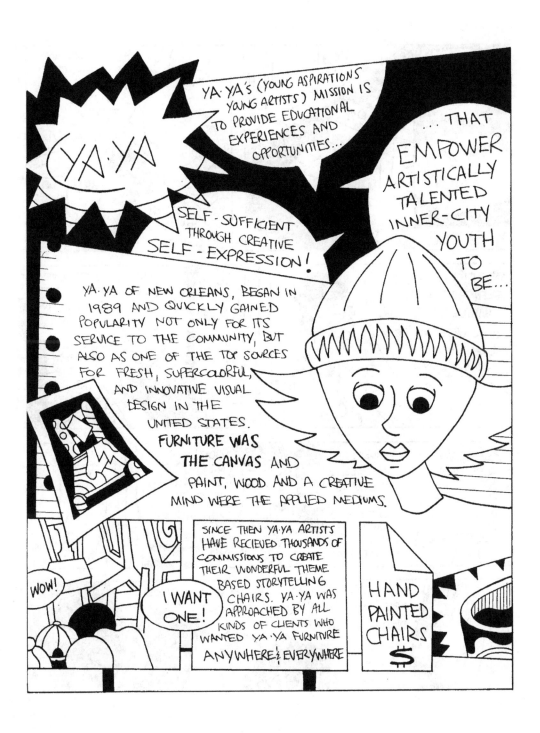

Art by Courtney Collins and Rondell Crier, copyright 2005

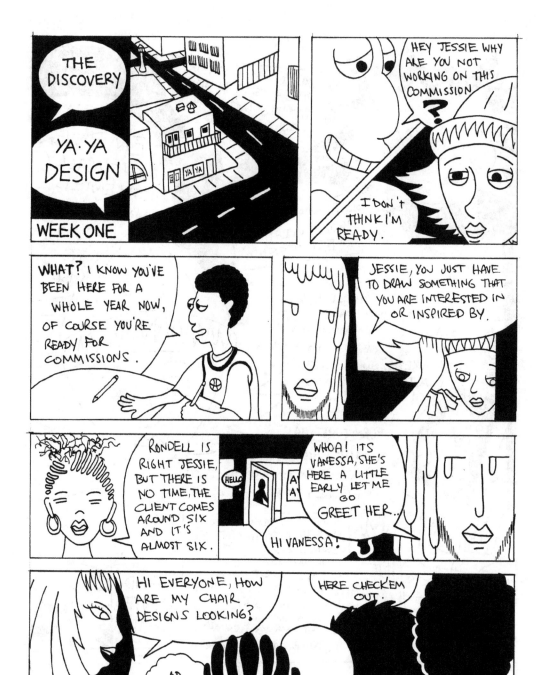

Art by Courtney Collins and Rondell Crier, copyright 2005

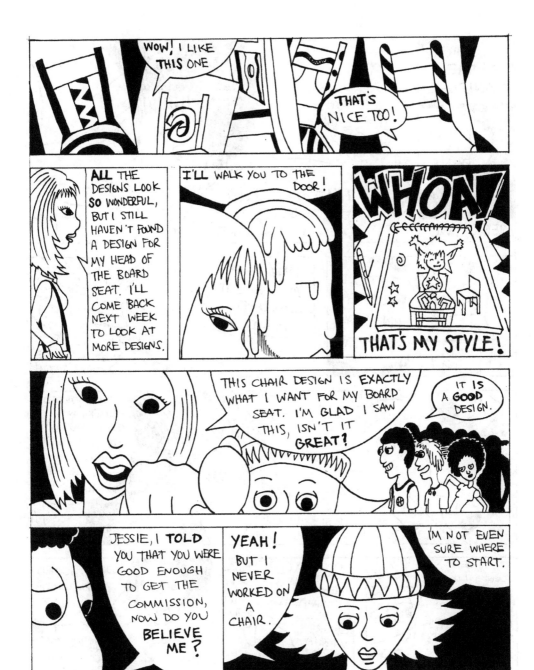

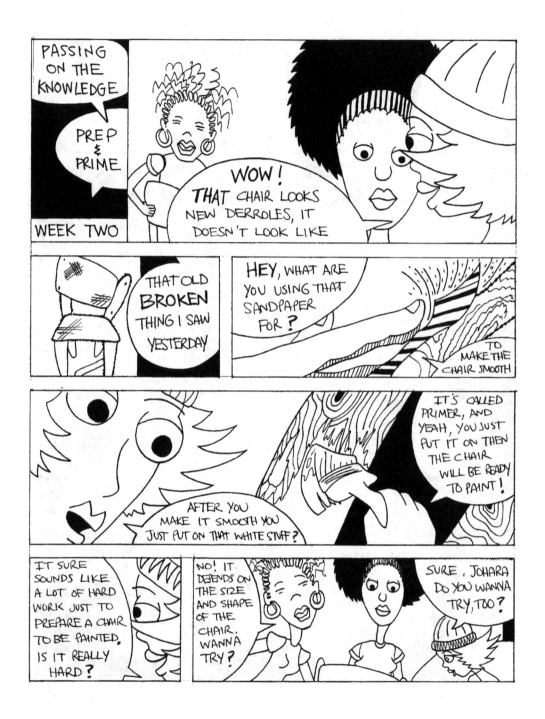

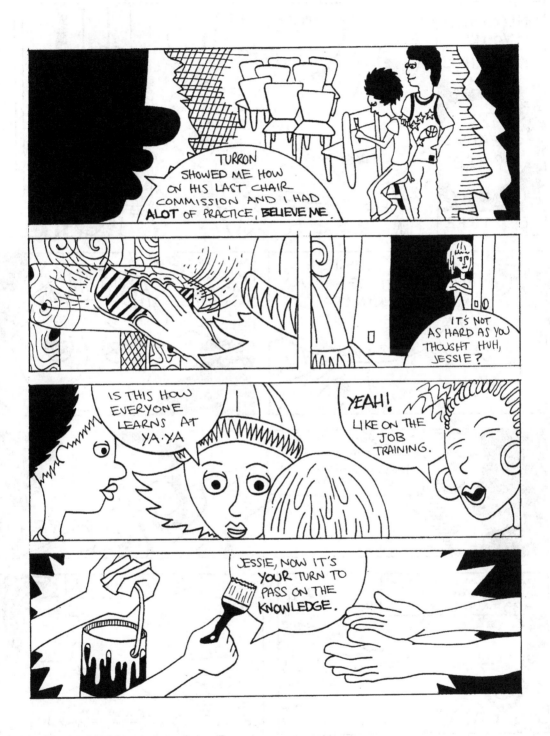

Art by Courtney Collins and Rondell Crier, copyright 2005

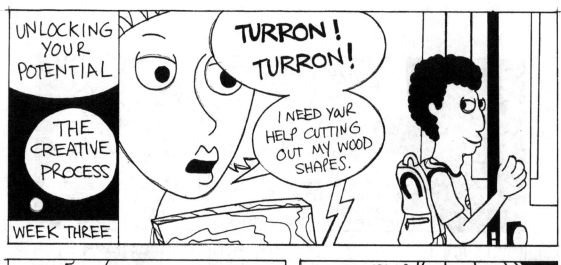

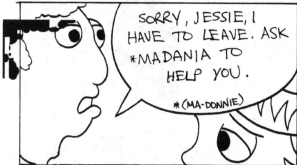

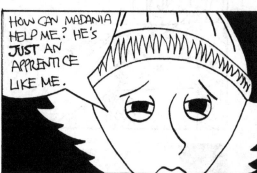

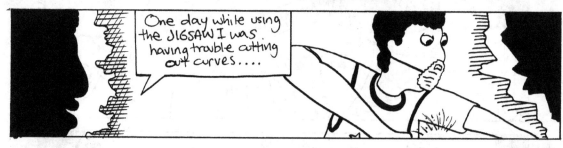

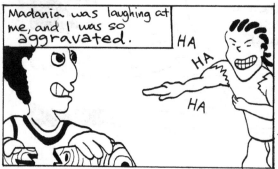

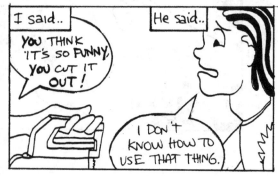

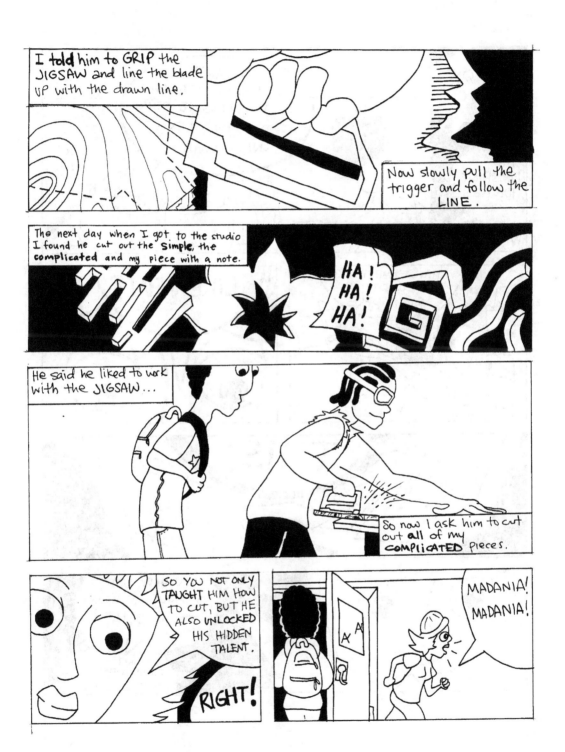

Art by Courtney Collins and Rondell Crier, copyright 2005

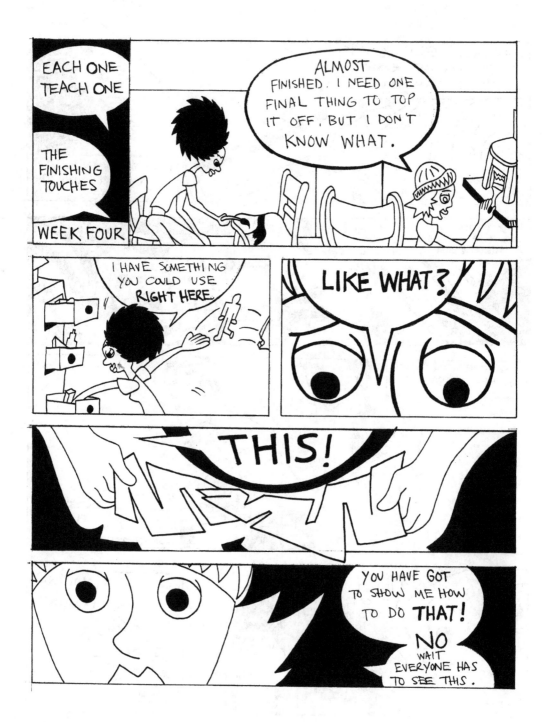

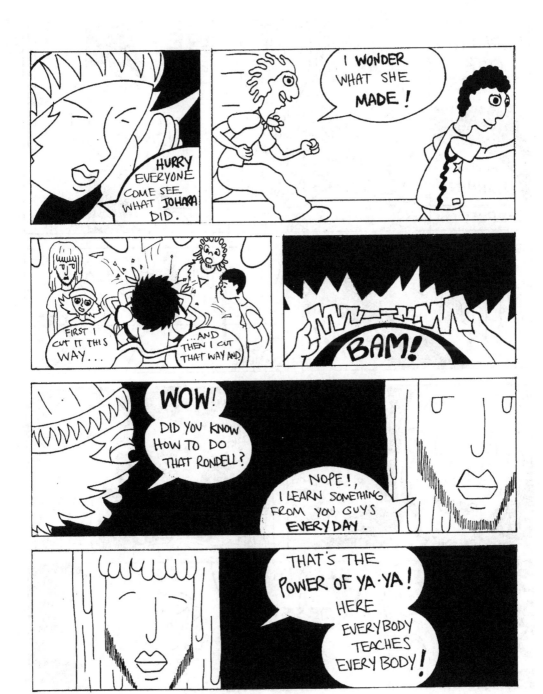

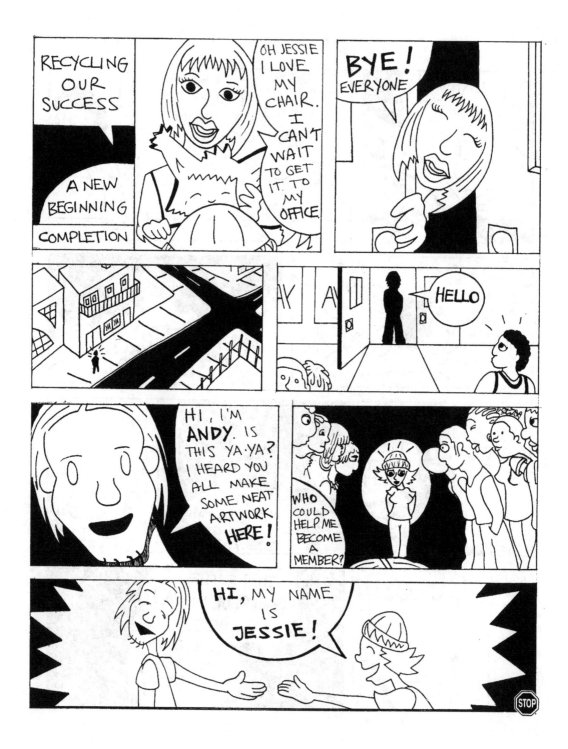

Art by Courtney Collins and Rondell Crier, copyright 2005

INSIDE THE CRAFT CIRCLE

TIP

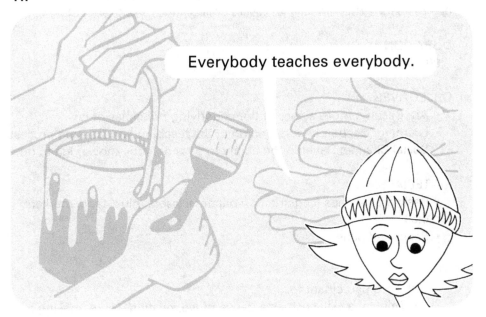

Everybody teaches everybody.

TOPICS

- How are teaching and learning inter-connected?
- What are the qualities of an effective teacher? Student?
- How can peer teaching be integrated throughout the CRAFT process?

TECHNIQUE: "EVERYBODY TEACHES EVERYBODY" EXERCISE

Derived from exercises of Young Aspirations / Young Artists, New Orleans, LA

DURATION
  90 minutes

OBJECTIVES
  • Art: Become more aware of the underlying principles of art.
  • Learning: Deepen understanding of the teaching and learning process.
  • Social Change: Develop the ability to pass on your knowledge to others.

MATERIALS
  • Basic art supplies (construction paper, scissors, glue, tape, markers, etc.)
  • Paper and pens

STEPS
  1. Ask each participant to:
     • Think of a skill such as a dance move, reciting a joke, making a folded paper hat, or drawing a logo.
     • Write 3 to 4 components of that skill, such as a sequence of steps, a style, timing, composition, etc.

  2. Divide the group into pairs.

  3. Allow 30 minutes for partners to:
     • Teach each other their skill and components.
     • Apply the same components of the newly acquired skill in a different way or with different content.

  4. Have pairs share their efforts with the larger group. Focus on learning, teaching, and interpreting skills used in the process.

VARIATIONS / FOLLOW-UP
  • Use this exercise for people to get acquainted at the beginning of a creative project.
  • Identify new skills learned at the end of a project.

BAGGAGE CLAIM

What a trip! We have visited so many different types of people responding to different kinds of challenges, and everywhere we went, we found people and places being transformed through art.

We met dancers and singers, potters and poets, outlaw truckers and shamans-in-training. We went from inside an ancient pueblo to the inside of a 21st century prison cell, and joined campaigns for economic development, community health, environmental conservation, criminal justice and grassroots democracy. In each story, we found common themes which can provide a new way to think about the creative process.

From birth to death, human beings respond to our world through the languages of art. We take the cultural materials given to us from the **past** and transform them in light of the **present**, with the goal of somehow making our **future** better. Humanity itself moves forward when the imaginings of one generation become part of the information available to the next. This is the impulse for democratic human progress, and it is at the heart of what it means to practice community-based art.

True democracy depends upon a growing number of us exercising our creative abilities. Anything that blocks creativity, be it poverty, illness, overwork, discrimination, distrust, inequality, violence – must be changed in order for us to move forward.

Signs, symbols, rituals and stories are not only an end, but also a means to spark the process of creative transformation. These cultural codes carry vital information, and they enable us to imagine alternatives. Through a process we are only now beginning to fully understand, art can stimulate the ability of people to work together creatively to solve common problems.

The people we visited on our journey are not superheroes, but they are performing heroic acts every day. They are tapping into the deepest wellsprings of human knowledge in order to help themselves, their communities and us all to create a better society.

> "Now the form of action is being determined, in which is contained, like the nucleus in the atom, the great enigma of the ends and the means. It's at this early point, at the crux of germination that the poet can turn the palindrome of *evil* into *live*."
>
> — JUDITH MALINA, CO-FOUNDER, THE LIVING THEATRE

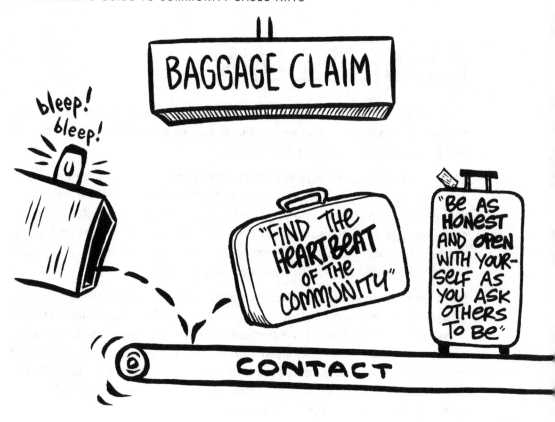

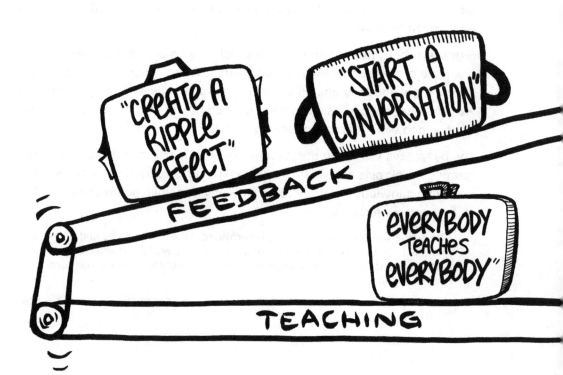

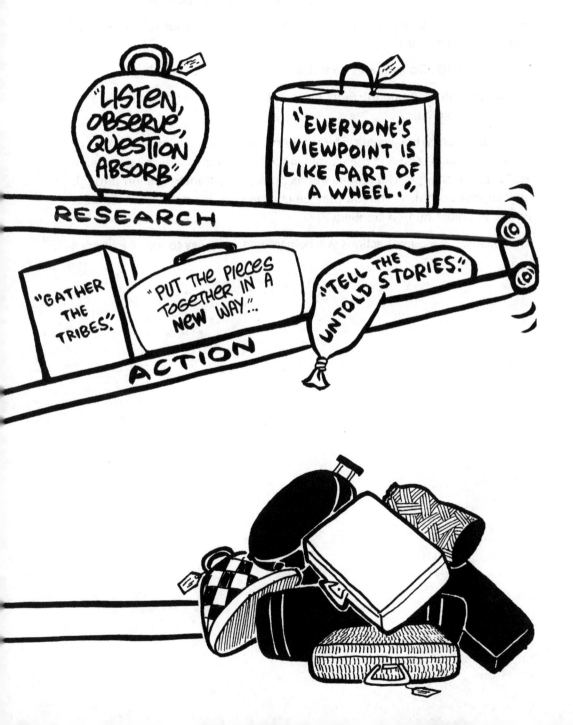

P.S. WHERE TO NEXT?

We appear to have come to an end of a journey, and perhaps the beginning of another one. Once again, the question is Where are you headed?

Having read this book, you are now at a crossroads in your relationship to community-based art.

BEGINNERS: Do I want to do this kind of work in the world?

VETERANS: Can I do my work better? How can I pass on what I have learned to others?

Every community has issues. The world needs people willing to be part of finding solutions. You and the people in your community can collaborate on art for social change. The stories in this book prove transformation through art happens everyday. The job may be challenging, but it comes with great power to unlock human creativity.

The following Resource sections will help you on your way to future journeys.

RESOURCES

TRAILBLAZERS

In order to understand the core concepts of the community-based arts movement (see Glossary for definitions), we sought the wisdom of these thinkers:

1. On **art**:

"The human species has had an evolutionary history of about 4 million years.
If we presume to speak about art history, we must take into account this entire
period." — BIOLOGIST ELLEN DISSANAYAKE

2. On **community**:

"Each community boasts a unique combination of assets upon which to build
its future. A thorough map of these assets would begin with an inventory of
the gifts, skills and capacities of the people who are part of that community."
— SOCIOLOGISTS JOHN P. KRETZMANN & JOHN L. MCKNIGHT

3. On **community-based art**:

"The motivation of aesthetic or creative activity is the impulse to make 'it' better, when 'it' is one's dynamic relationship to others.   In this sense, all art is
community-based."

— THEATER ARTIST/ACTIVIST JOHN O'NEAL

4. On **consensus**:

"Consensus is based on the belief that each person has some part of the truth
and no one has all of it..."

— QUAKER, AND MEETING FACILITATION TRAINER, CAROLYN ESTES

5. On **culture**:

"To truly know ourselves, it is necessary to not merely be in the cultural world
but to change it." — ANTHROPOLOGIST PAUL WILLIS

6. On **democracy**:

"Cultural democracy is predicated on the idea that diverse cultures should be
treated as essentially equal in our multicultural societies. Within this framework, cultural development becomes a process of assisting communities and
individuals to learn, express and communicate in multiple directions, not
merely from the top down.

— CULTURAL PLANNERS/SCHOLARS DON ADAMS & ARLENE GOLDBARD

CONTINUED

7. On **identity**:

"'Identity' as a phenomenon of human consciousness depends much more on how those in one's immediate environment ask questions, give directions, frame time and space, and reflect expectations, than it does on verbal declarations of collectivity or acceptance or on common labels."

— ANTHROPOLOGIST SHIRLEY BRICE HEATH AND
EDUCATOR MILBREY W. MCLAUGHLIN

8. On **learning**:

"There is no teaching without learning. Both take place in such a way that those who teach learn, on the one hand, because they recognize previously learned knowledge and, on the other, because by observing how the novice student's curiosity works to apprehend what is taught, they help themselves to uncover uncertainties, rights and wrongs."   — EDUCATOR PAULO FREIRE

9. On **objectives**:

"When I think of the future, I think of ...a society where many peoples can live and share the same world without killing, exploiting and ruling each other. Whenever I consider my objectives in a particular situation, it is that vision which drives my efforts."

— SINGER/SCHOLAR BERNICE JOHNSON REAGON

10. On **partnership** (also known as collaboration):

"Nobody does anything by themselves in an institutional or community setting. Giving and gaining respect make it possible to build the relationships required to operate effectively in these places."

— ARTS ADVOCATE BILL CLEVELAND

11. On **power**:

"Without power, there is no social change. Each of us needs to discover and exercise the power within us that enabled Rosa Parks to choose not to go to the back of the bus without waiting to see if others would join her."
— ACTIVIST GRACE LEE BOGGS

12. On **people power**:

Your task, actors, is to be
Explorers and teachers of the art of dealing with people,
Knowing their nature and demonstrating it you teach people
To deal with themselves. You teach them the great art
Of living together.   — POET/PLAYWRIGHT BERTOLT BRECHT

13. On **social change**:

"True social change is a never-ending process. Our alliances and our sense of historical continuity create the binding solidarities that are our greatest defense in the battle for social justice."

— VISUAL ARTIST/SCHOLAR AMALIA MESA BAINS

ARTIST PROFILES

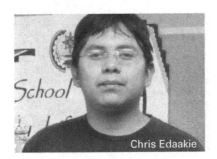

Chris Edaakie

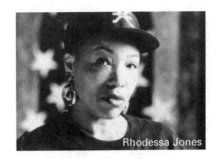

Rhodessa Jones

I-AM-GOING-BUT-I-SHALL-RETURN Pages 5–17

ARTIST	Christopher Edaakie
ORGANIZATION	School Healthy Lifestyles
HOME	Zuni Pueblo, New Mexico
MISSION	To create a bridge between the young and the old, the past and the present, to remember our proud heritage and to use this to keep our people strong and healthy.
ADVICE	During this lifetime, learn as much of your roots as possible, know where you come from. Our elders are like a great library, respect them and learn from them. Use this knowledge to help others find their place in this world.

MORE THAN AEROBICS Pages 18–28

ARTIST	Rhodessa Jones
ORGANIZATION	Cultural Odyssey (sponsor of the Medea Project)
HOME	San Francisco, CA
MISSION	To address the cultural and social needs of the female incarcerated population.
ADVICE	It is not enough to want to "do" community-based art. You have to come to understand this work as an act of survival for yourself and the communities you hope to serve. Be interested in all people and all things … they are your mentors.
URL	www.culturalodyssey.org

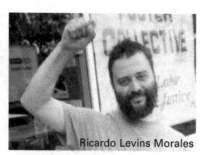

Ricardo Levins Morales

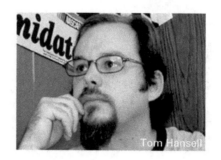

Tom Hansell

VISUAL GRIOT   Pages 31–42

ARTIST	Ricardo Levins Morales
ORGANIZATION	RLM Arts Studio
HOME	Minneapolis, MN
MISSION	To help create a global culture based on love rather than greed as its operating principle.
ADVICE	It's important that people feel you are with them in spirit – not just a technician for hire. Be honest about what's most important to you and what kind of artist you want to be. Many hands will help you get there.
URL	www.rlmartstudio.com

COAL BUCKET OUTLAW   Pages 43–57

ARTIST	Tom Hansell
ORGANIZATION	Appalshop
HOME	Whitesburg, KY
MISSION	To document, disseminate and revitalize the creativity and traditions of Appalachian communities, and in so doing, support these communities' efforts to achieve justice and equity.
ADVICE	Make time for listening and for surprises. It is easy to fall into the trap of "selling" yourself or your work to a community. Simply hang out with people and learn about their personal interests and challenges.
URL	www.appalshop.org

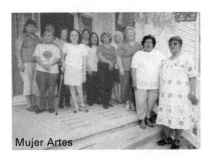

Mujer Artes

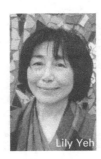

Lily Yeh

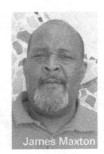

James Maxton

COMADRES Pages 61–73

ARTIST	Mujer Artes Ceramics Cooperative
ORGANIZATION	Esperanza Peace & Justice Center
HOME	San Antonio, TX
MISSION	To enable women of Mexican descent to explore their creative skills, develop their creative voices and bring their art to the community.
ADVICE	It is through shared life experiences and traditions that a bond of goodwill is created between the artist and community. Through art, you learn there are no limits; with the mind you collaborate, and with the hands you construct.
URL	www.esperanzacenter.org

THAT LUMINOUS PLACE Pages 74–88

ARTIST	Lily Yeh and James Maxton
ORGANIZATION	Village of Arts & Humanities
HOME	Philadelphia
MISSION	To build community through innovative arts, educational, social, construction, and economic development programs.
ADVICE	Our ability to unlock the creativity and dreams of community residents, to reframe deficits as resources, and to channel energy into results-oriented projects, are the keys to our approach. Our success is due in large part to the enthusiasm, support and participation of committed community members.
URL	www.villagearts.org

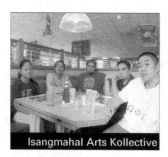

Isangmahal Arts Kollective

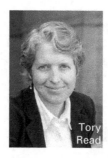

Tory Read

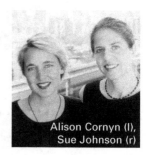

Alison Cornyn (l), Sue Johnson (r)

ONE LOVE Pages 89–100

ARTISTS	Jojo Gaon, Angela Dy, Daps, Hoven Vida, Grace Antonio, plus many others
ORGANIZATION	Isangmahal Arts Kollective
HOME	Seattle, WA
MISSION	To express and analyze through our art the problems of life that we all share. To propagate LOVE, the sole basis of life and all revolutions.
ADVICE	Find your self through your art and the process of art in life. Don't get caught up in the unnecessary details of the process, but do get caught up in the scenery. Love is love.

TALK BACK Pages 103–116

ARTIST	Tory Read
ORGANIZATION	Greenpeace International
HOME	Oakland, CA (previously Denver)
MISSION	To create a lyrical, multi-voice, photo-text record of our moment in history by recording the stories of people and places that are overlooked by mainstream media.
ADVICE	Make art and share it with your friends. Find a teacher. Practice. Use your voice. Have fun. Don't let negative people get you down. Express yourself even when people don't like it.
URL	www.community-photography.com

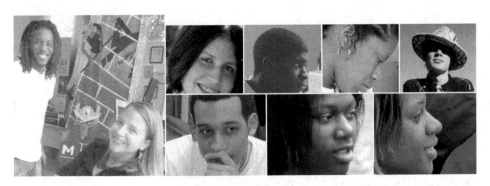

YA/YA. Far left: Rondell Crier and Ann Schieders. Inset, clockwise from upper left: Jessie, Courtney, Derroles, Andy, Madania, Johara, Turron.

TOWN HALL IN CYBERSPACE Pages 117–129

ARTIST	Alison Cornyn, Sue Johnson
ORGANIZATION	360 Degrees
HOME	New York City / World Wide Web
MISSION	To use technology to empower people for justice and democracy. To create spaces (online and off) for people to share stories and experiences around major social issues.
ADVICE	Let people know what you are working on. Get your friends involved to transform something they feel is not right. Begin to envision what it is that you would like to see happening.
URL	www.picture-projects.com; www.360degrees.org

JESSIE'S STORY Pages 133–146

ORGANIZATION	Young Aspirations / Young Artists
HOME	New Orleans, LA
MISSION	To provide experiences and opportunities that empower talented inner-city youth to be professionally self-sufficient through creative self-expression.
ADVICE	Don't overlook or underestimate the power of youth. Given the right tools and a supportive environment, motivated young people can do extraordinary things.
URL	www.yayainc.com

LINKS TO THE FIELD

The field of community-based arts in the United States is constantly growing and changing. We offer here a few key online resources to help beginners join in!

ALLIED MEDIA PROJECTS (www.alliedmedia.org)
A national network of media makers, artists, educators, and technologists working for social justice.

ALTERNATE ROOTS (www.alternateroots.org)
A regional arts service organization with over 300 members and 39 years of history in arts and social justice work in the South.

BEAUTIFUL TROUBLE (www.beautifultrouble.org)
A book, web toolbox and international network of artist-activist trainers whose mission is to make grassroots movements more creative and more effective.

COMMUNITY ARTS NETWORK (www.tinyurl.com/y7p7kpoj)
An archive of articles, essays and other resources about community-based arts projects published from 1999 to 2010.

C.R.A.F.T. CIRCLE (www.thecraftcircle.org)
A national learning community of teachers, teaching artists and organizers that work with young people and use the C.R.A.F.T. methodology.

HIGHLANDER CENTER (www.highlandercenter.org)
A catalyst for grassroots organizing and movement building in Appalachia and the South through popular education, participatory research and cultural work.

IMAGINING AMERICA (www.imaginingamerica.org)
A consortium of colleges, universities and organizations that strengthen the public roles of the arts, humanities, and design through research, action, and leadership development.

NATIONAL GUILD FOR COMMUNITY ARTS EDUCATION (www.nationalguild.org)
A service organization for community schools of the arts, arts centers and arts education departments in institutions, universities and museums in 45 states.

TEACHER ACTIVIST GROUPS (www.teacheractivistgroups.org)
A national coalition of local teacher organizing groups that engage in shared political education and relationship building.

TEACHING TOLERANCE (www.tolerance.org)
A project of the Southern Poverty Law Center, the website features great resources for social justice teachers, including a magazine, blog and classroom resources.

U.S. DEPARTMENT OF ARTS & CULTURE (www.usdac.us)
A people-powered, grassroots action network that uses creativity and social imagination to shape a shared culture of empathy, equity, and belonging.

CRAFT ACTIVITIES TABLE

CRAFT originated as part of the East Bay Institute for Urban Arts, a program for teens based in Oakland, CA, from 1994 to 2001. Urban Arts and the CRAFT framework grew out of the organizing approach of the Center for Third World Organizing (www.ctwo.org). The table below provides a distillation of community-based arts activities, showing how INFORMATION, IMAGINATION, and ACTION can take place in each of the CRAFT territories.

	ART Sample Activities	**ACADEMIC LEARNING** Sample Activities	**SOCIAL CHANGE** Sample Activities
Contact Cultivate trust, mutual understanding and commitment as a foundation for your creative partnership.	• Cultural Inventory • Cultural Jeopardy • Genres and Issues	• Surface prior knowledge through polls, interviews and observations. • Present and discuss the common core standard.	• Request assistance from a community-based organization. • Negotiate agreement.
Research Gather information about the people, places and issues you are working with.	• Host Story Circles with community members.	• Gather perspectives through polls, interviews and observations. • Present and discuss key concepts and histories.	• Attend community organizing meetings and events on the issue
Action Produce a new work of art that benefits the community.	• Develop, refine and produce one or more artistic products or events.	• Analyze the art and the issue through the production of a program guide.	• Premiere the new art and guidebook for issue stakeholders and peers
Feedback Spark reflection, dialogue and organizing to spread the impact of the new work.	• Facilitate audience feedback sessions using the Critical Response Format.© • Use feedback to refine work.	• Gather and analyze feedback through polls, interviews and observations. • Use feedback to refine work.	• Reproduce and distribute the new art to benefit organizing efforts. • Use feedback to refine work.
Teaching Pass on skills to sustain the impact.	• Lead peer-to-peer workshops based upon the project artwork.	• Produce portfolios that document and justify academic learning.	• Participate in community event to celebrate and learn from the experience.

SAMPLE CRAFT PROGRAM DESIGN

PROGRAM ACTIVITIES
Community Arts Apprenticeship Program 1999
Theme: Environmental Justice

Week One: Contact
- Objectives: Introduce participants and theme, Set goals, Agree on guidelines for collaboration.
- Culminating activity: the group creates an environmental street performance/installation for mid-day on Friday at an active downtown site.

	Monday	Tuesday	Wednesday	Thursday	Friday
Warm-ups 9:00 – 9:30	Orientation Warm-ups	Orientation Warm-ups	Warm-ups	Warm-ups	Warm-ups at City Center
Environ. Education 9:30 – 10:30	Connections between class, race and pollution	Story Circles about the environment	"Water and Power" group game*	Arts Production groups work on mini-projects	Street Performance/ Installation Get feedback from audience.
Small groups 10:45 – Noon	Cultural Inventory	Create Journals Set personal/ professional goals	Create list of speakers from the community related to goals		
Lunch Noon – 2:00	Open Studios	Open Studios	Open Studios	Open Studios	Open Studios
Arts Production 2:00 – 3:45	Assess skills, Thumbnails** exercise	Brainstorm ideas for mini-project based on stories	Develop ideas for mini-projects	Finish and share mini-projects	Debrief from experience. Use CRAFT map.
3:45 – 4:00			Closing		

* The "Water and Power" game, created by Ariel Luckey, demonstrates the links between health and privilege using a race between teams with unequal resources.

** "Thumbnails" are small group improvisations based on random combinations of cultural codes (themes) and artistic disciplines (formats).

Urban Arts developed skills in both the arts (theater, photography, painting and music) and community organizing. Each year, about 40 teens and 8 adults were involved in a 6-week summer program, culminating in a series performance-installation events. Each year there was a different social change theme, sometimes very specific, such as a ballot initiative about city budget policy, and sometimes very general (e.g. Family).

This sample program design is from the Summer 1999 program, when the theme was Environmental Justice. The group testified at public hearings, performed at rallies and created a play ("Toxic City") that raised community awareness about a low technology medical waste incinerator causing dioxin poisoning in East Oakland neighborhoods. The play helped a community coalition force a shut down and an upgrade of the incinerator.

The complete program takes place over a six-week period. Each week follows the CRAFT sequence, moving from Contact through Research, Action, Feedback and Teaching.

CREDITS

These are the artists, photographers and researchers whose work we have used in the book.

COVER
Illustrations by Keith Knight, Ellen Forney. Graphic Design by Christine Wong Yap.

DEDICATION PAGE
Photo by El Sawyer, courtesy of Village of Arts and Humanities.

Preface, p.ix
p. ix. Illustrations by Keith Knight, Ellen Forney
p. x. From left: Poster courtesy of Ricardo Levins Morales, Northland Poster Collective. Photo courtesy of Cultural Odyssey's archives. Video still courtesy of Appalshop.

PACKING FOR THE TRIP
Greetings, p. xiii
p. xiv. Clockwise from left: Photo © Travis Ness, Istockphoto. Photo by Kim Dummons. Photo by Jeff Whetstone, courtesy of Appalshop. Photo by Alex Lubin. Photo by Mat Schwarzman.
Meet Me at the Crossroads, p. xv
Farris Thompson, Robert, *Flash of the Spirit: African & Afro-American Art & Philosophy*, Random House, 1983.
Mahdi, Louise Carus, Nancy Geyer Christopher and Michael Meade, editors, *Crossroads: The Quest for Contemporary Rites of Passage*, Open Court Publishing Company, 1996.
A New Look, p. xviii
PREMISE #1: CREATIVITY IS A MUSCLE
Boal, Augusto, *Theatre of the Oppressed*, Theatre Communications Group, 1979.
Darwin, Charles, *Origin of Species*, Gramercy, 1995.
Greene, Maxine, *Releasing the Imagination: Essays on Education, the Arts, and Social Change*, Jossey-Bass, 2000.
p. xix. From left: Photo © Kemie Guaida, Istockphoto. Photo © Martin Kawalski, Istockphoto.

PREMISE #2: ART IS INFORMATION
hooks, bell, *Yearning: race, gender, and cultural politics*, South End Press, 1990.
Lippard, Lucy, *Mixed Blessings: New Art in a Multicultural America*, Pantheon Books, 1990.
McCloud, Scott, *Understanding Comics*, Perennial Currents, 1994.
p. xx. Clockwise from upper left: Photo © Ahmed Hussam, Istockphoto. Comic reproduced with permission of Keith Knight. Painting by Eugene Delacroix, "Liberty Leading the People," 1830. Photo © Jody Elliott, Istockphoto.
p. xxi. From left: Photo © Ana Abejon, Istockphoto. Photo © David M. Albrecht, Istockphoto. Photo © Sharon Dominick, Istockphoto.

PREMISE #3 COMMUNITIES ARE CULTURES
Florida, Richard, T*he Rise of the Creative Class: And How It's Transforming Work, Leisure, Community and Everyday Life*, Basic Books, 2004.
Gladwell, Malcolm, *The Tipping Point: How Little Things Can Make a Big Difference*, Back Bay Books, 2002.
McAdam, Doug, "Culture and Social Movements" in Laraña, Enrique, Hank Johnston and Joseph R. Gusfield, editors, *New Social Movements: From Ideology to Identity*, Temple University Press, 1994, pp. 36-57.
p. xxii. Photo by Lonny Shavelson/ photowords.com
p. xxiii. Photo by Lonny Shavelson/ photowords.com
p. xxiv. Photo © Brand X Pictures.

TALES FROM THE ROAD

CONTACT
I-Am-Going-But-I-Shall-Return
p. 5. Clockwise from upper left: Photo by Alex Lubin. Photo © Salvador Hernandez, Istockphoto. Photo by Virginia Giglio, PhD, Global Thinking, Inc. Photo by Alex Lubin.

p. 6. From top: Photo by Albert Chopito, courtesy of Chris Edaakie / Healthy Lifestyles. Poster courtesy of Chris Edaakie / Healthy Lifestyles. Photo by Melissa Vicenti courtesy of Chris Edaakie / Healthy Lifestyles.

pp. 7–14. Graphic Storyteller: Keith Knight.

More Than Aerobics

p. 18. From Top: Photo by Robert Vente. Photo © Amy Yang, Istockphoto.

p. 19. From Top: Photo by Scott Braley. Photo courtesy of Cultural Odyssey's archives.

pp. 20–26. Graphic Storyteller: Keith Knight.

RESEARCH

Visual Griot

p. 31. Top: Photo by Chris Gregerson. Bottom, from left: Photo courtesy of National Archives and Records Administration. Photo © Michael Siluk.

p. 32. Posters courtesy of Ricardo Levins Morales, Northland Poster Collective.

pp. 33–39. Graphic Storyteller: Keith Knight.

Coal Bucket Outlaw

p. 43. Photos by Hope Frazier.

p. 44. Photo by Jeff Whetstone, courtesy of Appalshop.

pp. 45–54. Graphic Storyteller: Ellen Forney.

ACTION

Comadres

p. 61. From top: Photo © David M. Albrecht, Istockphoto. Photo by Jim West.

p. 62. Photo by Miguel Gonzales. Photo by Mimi Zarsky. Photo by Miguel Gonzales.

p. 63–70. Graphic Storyteller: Ellen Forney.

That Luminous Place

p. 74. From top: Photo © Gary Lambert / Istockphoto. Photo by Greg Heller. Photo by Rob Lamb, courtesy of the Village of Arts and Humanities.

p. 75. Top: Photo by Rob Lamb, courtesy of the Village of Arts and Humanities. Bottom: Photos by Keith Knight.

pp. 76–85. Graphic Storyteller: Keith Knight.

One Love

p. 89. From top: Photo © Travis Ness, Istockphoto. Photo from the James Earl Wood collection of photographs relating to Filipinos in California, BANC PIC 1945.010, courtesy of the Bancroft Library, University of California, Berkeley.

p. 90. Photos © Isangmahal Arts Kollective, courtesy of Jojo Gaon.

pp. 91–97. Graphic Storyteller: Ellen Forney.

FEEDBACK

Talk Back

p. 103. From top: "Teen Shot in Car at Notorious Corner" by John C. Ensslin, *Rocky Mountain News*, Feb. 17, 1995. Reprinted with permission of the *Rocky Mountain News*. Photo: Photodisc / Getty Images. Photo by Brenda Quinn.

p. 104. From top: "Boy Shot in Curtis Park Dies" by John C. Ensslin, *Rocky Mountain News*, February 18, 1995. Reprinted with permission of the *Rocky Mountain News*. Photo by David Grinspoon. Photo by Tory Read. "Residents' neighborhood photos speak eloquently of realities, joys" by Jeff Bradley, *Denver Post,* April 21, 1998. Reprinted with permission.

pp. 105–113. Graphic Storyteller: Keith Knight.

Town Hall in Cyberspace

p. 117. From top: Illustration courtesy of Picture Projects. Photos 1 & 2 by Scott Braley.

p. 118. From top: Photo: Photodisc / Getty Images. Screenshots courtesy of Picture Projects.

p. 119–126. Graphic Storyteller: Keith Knight.

TEACHING

Jessie's Story

p. 133. Photos 1 & 2 by Stanley Beck. Photo by Rick Olivier.

p. 134. Top row, from left: Logo courtesy of Pieces of Power. Logo courtesy of Tipitina's Foundation. Logo courtesy of Bamboula 2000. Center row: Art courtesy of Young Aspirations / Young Artists.

pp. 135–144. Graphic Storytellers: Courtney Collins, Rondell Crier.

Baggage Claim

pp. 148-149. Illustration by Ellen Forney, Keith Knight.

CONTINUED

RESOURCES

Trailblazers

On art: Dissanayake, Ellen, *What Is Art For?*, University of Washington Press, 1990, p. 5.

On community: Kretzmann, John P. and John L. McKnight, *Building Communities From the Inside Out: A Path Towards Finding and Mobilizing a Community's Assets*, ACTA Publications, 1997, p. 6.

On community-based art: O'Neal, John, "The Thing About Criticism," in O'Brien, Mark and Craig Little, editors, *Reimaging America: The Arts of Social Change*, New Society Publishers, 1990, p. 201.

On consensus: Estes, Carolyn, "Consensus," *In Context, A Quarterly Of Humane Sustainable Culture*, Autumn 1984, page 19.

On culture: Willis, Paul, *Common Culture: Symbolic Work at Play in the Everyday Cultures of the Young*, Westview Press, 1990, p. 22.

On democracy: Adams, Don & Arlene Goldbard, *Creative Community: The Art of Cultural Development*, Rockefeller Foundation, 2001, p.55.

On identity: Brice Heath, Shirley and Milbrey McLaughlin, editors, *Identity & Inner-City Youth: Beyond Ethnicity and Gender*, Teachers College Press, 1993, p. 8.

On learning: Freire, Paulo, *Teachers as Cultural Workers: Letters to Those Who Dare Teach*, Westview Press, 1998, p. 17.

On objectives: Reagon, Bernice, "Nurturing Resistance" in O'Brien, Mark and Craig Little, editors, *Reimaging America: The Arts of Social Change,* New Society Publishers, 1990, p. 5.

On partnership: Cleveland, William, *Art in Other Places: Artists at Work in America's Community and Social Institutions,* Praeger Publishers, 1992, p. 7.

On power: Boggs, Grace Lee, "These are the times that try our Souls," published online at www.communityarts.net.

On people power: Brecht, Bertolt, "Speech to Danish Working Class Actors on the Art of Observation," translation from *Poems,* *1913-1956,* edited by Willet, John and Ralph Mannheim, p. 237.

On social change: Mesa Bains, Amalia, from an interview with the author; and "A Model of Arts, Justice and Community" by Amalia Mesa Bains and Richard Bains, in *Social Justice: A Journal of Crime, Conflict and World Order*, Vol 29, No 4., editors Katz, Susan and Cecilia O'Leary.

Artist profiles

p. 153. From left: Photo by Alex Lubin. Photo by Diane McCurty, courtesy of Cultural Odessey's archives.

p. 154. From left: Photo by Mat Schwarzman. Photo by Rhonda Simpson, courtesy of Tom Hansell.

p. 155. From left: Photo by Miguel Gonzales. Photo courtesy of the Village of Arts and Humanities. Photo of James Maxton by El Sawyer, courtesy of the Village of Arts and Humanities.

p. 156. From left: Photo courtesy of Isangmahal Arts Kollective. Photo by David Grinspoon, courtesy of Tory Read. Photo by Greg Vore, courtesy of Picture Projects.

p. 157. From left: Photo by Cheryl Gerber. Photos by YA/YA staff, courtesy of YA/YA.

BACK COVER

Knight photo by Ken Milburn.
Schwarzman photo by Rick Olivier.

ACKNOWLEDGMENTS

Our gratitude goes out to the many individuals and organizations who helped all along the way. May the road continue to open up before you, and the wind remain at your back!

National Advisors

Ron Bechet
Linda Frye Burnham
Brian Freeman
Maria Rosario Jackson
Waldo Martin
Lawrence Rinder
Jane Tenenbaum
Kathleen Tyner
MK Wegmann

Local Advisors

Claudia Barker
Carol Bebelle
John Fulwiler
Denise Pilie
Kathy Randels

Funders

Ford Foundation
Greater New Orleans Foundation
Nathan Cummings Foundation
National Endowment for the Arts
National Performance Network, with funds provided by the Doris
    Duke Charitable Foundation
Louisiana Division of the Arts
Arts Council of New Orleans
Needmor Fund
RosaMary Foundation
Patrick F. Taylor Foundation
Time Warner

Partners

Partner organizations provided fiscal sponsorship, in-kind resources and much-needed creative space for the guidebook to be developed.
Center for Digital Storytelling (2000)
National Performance Network (2001 – 2005)
Xavier University of Louisiana (2004 – 2005)

Thanks!

The 18 artists, educators, activists and teens who read and gave feed-back on the draft manuscript. The 300+ teens and adults of Urban Arts. Alternate ROOTS (Regional Organization of Theaters South), the California Institute for Integral Studies (where the book began as a doctoral dissertation), the Center for Third World Organizing, especially Rinku Sen. The extensive New Orleans support network, including 25 teachers and artists of the local collaborative inquiry group, plus Students at the Center, Jan Clifford, Lisa McCarthy, Stanlyn Breve, Therese Wegmann, June Wilson, Carol Durand, Valera Francis, Patricia Sills, Musicians & Artists Supporting Education, Douglass Community Coalition, Frederick A. Douglass High School, and Donna's Bar & Grill. Thanks to MaPo Kinnord-Payton, Gayle Isa and Sonia BashSheva Mañjon for pushing for theory. Thanks to Vanessa Whang, Joe Lambert and Nina Mullen, first to support this project. Also, big thanks to James Kass (San Francisco/Seattle), Edward Wemytewa (Zuni Pueblo), Rene Saenz (San Antonio), Kelly Tannen (Philadelphia) and Kathie DeNobriga (Atlanta).

Special Thanks!

Web host Greg Elin. Research assistants Erin Genrich, Shana Sassoon, and Jonathan Jones. Editorial consultant Ana Daboo. Researchers Troy Gooden, Betsy Raasch-Gilman, Kimberlye Hunicke and Alex Lubin. Elders in the movement who gave advice, ideas and shelter, including Howard Zinn, Lucy Lippard, Liz Lerman, Tomás Ybarra Frausto, Elizabeth Kasl, Dudley Cocke, Ted Berger, Michael Nash, John T. Scott, John Malpede and especially John O'Neal.

Extra Special Thanks!

Mark O'Brien, for the book *Reimaging America: The Arts of Social Change*, the underlying source for much of this book.

Lynne Elizabeth and Karen Kearney at New Village Press, for believing in the importance of the *Beginner's Guide*.

The 47 individual donors (friends, family members, colleagues) for keeping the project alive.

Our spouses, Kerstin Knight and Mimi Zarsky, for their unwavering support in the completion of this project.

BIOS

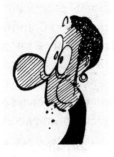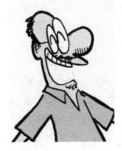

KEITH KNIGHT
Lead Graphic Journalist

Keith Knight is a homeschooling dad, a social activist, and an award-winning, nationally syndicated cartoonist. His work appears in the *Washington Post*, the *San Francisco Chronicle*, Daily Kos, Fusion, MAD Magazine and more. He is a 2015 recipient of a Belle Foundation grant and was named an NAACP History Maker for his compelling cartoon slideshow on police brutality called "They Shoot Black People, Don't They?" He lives in Carrboro, North Carolina. www.kchronicles.com

MAT SCHWARZMAN
Lead Author

Mat Schwarzman is a theater artist, educator, husband, dog parent and little brother. He holds a doctorate from California Institute for Integral Studies, where he focused on the transformative impact of the arts, education and community organizing on teenagers. Through his teaching, writing and theater work, he has reached thousands of youth and adults across the United States and beyond. He lives in New Orleans, where he has taught and lectured at Xavier University of Louisiana since 2003.

CONTINUED

Bill Cleveland, Editor William Cleveland is an internationally prominent writer, musician and Director of the Center for the Study of Art and Community. He has directed and consulted on cutting edge arts programs for teens, inmates and the general public throughout the United States for decades. His New Village Press book, *Art and Upheaval*, documents the efforts of artists working to help resolve conflict, promote peace, and rebuild civil society in communities in crisis around the world: www.artandcommunity.com

Courtney Collins and Rondell Crier, Guest Graphic Journalists (YA/YA) Courtney Collins has been a YA/YA participant since 2001 and is enrolled at Savannah College of Art and Design. Rondell Crier, while a YA/YA participant '91-'96, designed for Swatch and United Nations, and represented YA/YA in Japan, Germany, Italy, Holland, and numerous cities around the United States. In 2002, Mr. Crier returned to YA/YA to serve as Executive Director of Programs in partnership with Executive Director of Business Operations, Ann Schnieders.

Kimberly Dummons, Research Assistant Dummons is a sculptor and printmaker currently teaching design as a visiting artist at Middle Tennessee State University. She has worked with national and internationally known artists, including New Orleans public artist John T. Scott. This "wrangler of details" and pack rat loves to read and enjoys teaching youth and adults alike. Assisted 2002-2004

Ellen Forney, Graphic Journalist Seattle cartoonist/illustrator Ellen Forney's work appears regularly in many publications, including *LA Weekly, The Stranger,* and *Nickelodeon Magazine.* Her book of autobiographical comic strips, *Monkey Food: The Complete "I Was Seven in '75" Collection* was nominated for several national comics awards, and she has been teaching Comics at Cornish College of the Arts since 2002. She drives a silver 1968 Mercury Cougar, is a devoted swimmer and yoga practitioner, and has seen Laser Zeppelin three times. www.ellenforney.com

Bryan Jeffrey Graham, Website Designer Graham is sole proprietor of Big Tada Inc, a new design and production company focused on the arts and community development fields. Clients include New Orleans Museum of Art, National Performance Network, Greater New Orleans Afterschool Partnership, Center for Nonprofit Resources and the New Orleans Arts Exchange. A simple country boy from Chillicothe, Texas, Bryan remains committed to making his dream of performing a one-man *Evita* a reality. www.bigtada.com.

Marcia Lobman, Evaluation Coordinator Marcia Lobman has been designing, delivering and evaluating wide-ranging educational programs in her adopted state of Louisiana since 1970. Throughout her career, she has focused on assisting non-profit agencies to build and sustain effective educational programs for children and adults.

Christine Wong Yap, Art Director / Graphic Designer Christine Wong Yap is a graphic designer serving non-profit organizations. She is also an award-winning community muralist, and a painter and printmaker whose work has been exhibited locally and nationally. A longtime resident of Oakland, CA, she relocated to New York, NY in 2010. www.christinewongyap.com

Mimi Zarsky, Associate Producer Zarsky designs materials and produces events for nonprofit organizations. Currently on staff at the National Performance Network in New Orleans, her client list includes A Studio in the Woods, National Alliance for Media Arts and Culture, The San Francisco Foundation, Rockefeller Foundation and Junebug Productions. She appreciates a good story when she hears one, loves to cook, is a great dancer and a professional potter. Assisted 2003 - 2004

E-BOOK EDITION

Hoorah! Digitized format of the *Beginner's Guide to Community-Based Arts* is now available for most ebook reading devices. The E-Book edition can be ordered through ebook retailers and online through New Village Press **www.newvillagepress.net**

ISBN 978-1-61332-025-9

CROSSROADS COMICS!

Bring selected comics from the *Beginner's Guide* into your classroom or study circle with *Crossroads Comics*. Comics are sold individually for $5 or in teacher packs of 15 for $40 (prices do not include shipping and applicable sales tax). Discounts available for larger orders. *Crossroad Comics* can be ordered online through New Village Press **www.newvillagepress.net** or email hello@newvillagepress.net

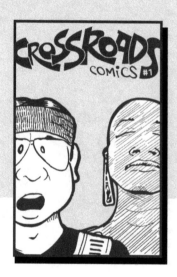

HELLO NEW VILLAGE PRESS!

You are holding a newly revised edition of one of the first and most popular books published by New Village Press, a unique public-benefit publisher serving the field of community building. Communities are where social change begins, and the healthiest, most creative changes spring from the grassroots. New Village Press began as a project of Architects/Designers/Planners for Social Responsibility (www.adpsr.org), an educational non-profit organization working for peace, environmental protection, social justice, and the development of healthy communities.

See what else we publish: **www.newvillagepress.net**

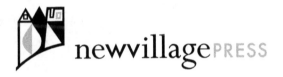